Ayrton Senna

Above and beyond

Ayrton Senna

Above and beyond

by

Pierre Menard & Jacques Vassal

Car profiles
Pierre Ménard

Photographs
LAT (unless stated otherwise)

Translated from french by
Eric Silbermann

Design and cover
Cyril Davillerd

Layout
Solange Amara, Cyril Davillerd

Contents

Chapter 1
Order and poverty

In 1960, the year Ayrton Senna da Silva was born in São Paulo, Brazil inaugurated its new federal capital, Brasilia, a sparkling and futuristic city built from nothing in the state of Goias at the source of four rivers: Tocantins, Parana, Sao Francisco and Corumba. Work had started in this deserted area in 1956, but four years later the city already boasted a population of 120,000. However, Rio de Janeiro, the capital since it took over the role from Sao Salvador in 1763, counted 3,400,000 inhabitants. What would they think in the Da Silva's home town of São Paulo, which had a similar population and a more vibrant style than Rio? It could have been a candidate to take over the role of capital city.

With its new capital and two huge cities, Brazil was undergoing a major demographic expansion, the population having grown from 50 to 70 million in the past decade. It was a young population with at least half living in towns. The people were dynamic and enterprising, but they were held back by an unstable economic and political situation and glaring social inequality. And, as far as Ayrton Senna's future career was concerned, they had far more important matters to deal with than motor racing. Not surprising when the sport was financially inaccessible and did not form part of the nation's psyche. In any case, football was the national obsession and the natural attractions of the weather and the beaches were far more alluring.

Brasilia was officially born on 21st April, a month to the day after Ayrton and 1960 also saw a very aggressive presidential election campaign. The country was in the grip of galloping inflation with the cost of living tripling between 1956 and 1961 and that was the main point for debate. The country had definitely modernised, but it was also deeply in debt under President Juscelino Kubitschek and Vice-President Joao Goulart, the former leader of the socialist party. In 1960, the three candidates from the presidency were General Lott, a former war minister under Kubitschek, Janio Quadros a former governor of São Paulo and Adhemar De Barros, then the mayor of São Paulo. It was the Conservative Quadros who was seen as the candidate for the "little man" who promised to reduce inflation and emerged victorious. It meant that a Paulista was now president of the country. The vice-president was elected in a later election and in a typically Brazilian compromise, that role went once again to the socialist Goulart. As he had promised, Quadros initiated a programme of non-alignment with the United States, refusing to boycott Cuba for example and establishing trade links with the Soviet Union. However, when it came to internal matters, he could not keep his promises. Inflation was still endemic and after seven months, Quadros stood down saying he did not have the means to implement his policies.

Troubled times followed as the country was plunged deeper into an economic crisis which was extremely tough on Brazil and its people. It led to military intervention and the installation of a dictatorial regime which lasted for many years. This was the Brazil in which the young Ayrton grew up.

When Quadros resigned, he was replaced as president by Goulart, in August 1961. He was a left wing politician who also owned a large agricultural property and he adopted a policy of agricultural reform, aimed at helping the poorer farmers. But the landowners, the right wing, the province governors and the army blocked his plans, on the way accusing Goulart of working for the Communists. The two sides dug in and in March 1964, the army revolted, overthrowing Goulart, who went into exile, replacing him with a retired Marshal, Humberto de Alencar Castelo Branco, by means of a congressional vote. Over the next six months, thousands of people were arrested, civil servants sacked, elected official dismissed on the pretext of "subversion" and "corruption" using the special powers which the new regime granted itself. Despite pompous speeches from its leaders, inflation galloped along and the country's debts mounted and the gulf between the haves and have-nots grew even bigger, in a country where the large rural population already suffered from malnutrition and illiteracy.

It was during this period from 1965 to '75 that Brazilian music began to enjoy huge popularity and commercial success. Great poets, authors and composers such as Chico Buarque, Vinicius de Moraes, Dorival Caymni and later, Gilberto Gil, Caetano Veloso, Milton Nascimento and Maria Bethania played an important and yet ambivalent role. On the one hand they were artists witnessing and sometimes resisting the oppression, on the other they were cultural ambassadors, while their record sales boosted the economy.

The difficult times in political, social and economic terms, while fascinating culturally, largely passed by the Senna family, including young Ayrton. When the military took over, he was just having his first go behind the wheel of a motorised toy Jeep. There were less opportunities to move up the social ladder in the city than in the town and the rich quarter was well separated from the poor. The black population was in the minority and by then, the future world champion's family already had a reasonably comfortable lifestyle.

In 1960, Brazil began a motorway construction programme and with no home grown industry, imported cars and trucks from abroad, from the States and Europe, particularly from Germany. There were factories building truck engines under license from Fiat, named FNM (Fabrica Nacional de Motors,) or "FENEME" as it was known in São Paulo where the Portuguese language is peppered with Italian. The fact that the railway system was in disarray only served to see more money spent on road freight. American companies like Willys Overland set up shop in Brazil. Volkswagen also arrived in

1953 to build and sell its popular Beetle. It was the weapon of choice for many amateur drivers who tuned them up to compete in rallies, usually run on dirt roads. At the start of the Sixties, a Beetle cost the equivalent of 25 to 30 months salary for the average worker, which is why the slightly cheaper 2 stroke DKW was more popular in Brazil. In order to develop the car market, subscription books were sold in which the owner would stick a stamp every month. Each week, a raffle was organised and one lucky winner would walk away with a brand new car. At the other end of the scale, the height of luxury for the very rich was the Mercedes 220 SE. From the French side, Renault built the Dauphine under license in the Willys Overland do Brasil factory, starting in 1959, although very few were seen on the streets of São Paulo. In the sixties, the Alpine-Renault A110 sports car was also built in Brazil, going by the name of the Interlagos. The numbers were small, but it was enough to generate a taste for competition with a few Brazilian amateurs and it was a regular in rallies and also on the circuit with which it shared its name, the brand new track built "Between the Lakes" in a suburb of São Paulo.

The skyscrapers which now block out the sky above São Paulo were just being built in 1960 and the smog clouds had appeared over a city which was now home to 3,200,000 inhabitants. It was the capital of the state which bore its name –some consolation for not being the national capital – but it was already the country's nerve centre of industry, economy and was home to its major universities. As an example, 90% of the electricity produced in Brazil came from São Paulo. 500 kilometres to the south west of Rio, with which it enjoyed a frenetic rivalry, 80 kilometres from the port of Santos, with its beautiful beaches, São Paulo was the perfect breeding ground for future champions.

When the young Ayrton headed for the brand new circuit of Interlagos, just forty five

minutes from the family home, he was privileged enough to go there by car; chauffeur driven no less! The young poor, in other words the majority, who wanted to go there to spectate had to put up with a two hour journey by bus, when they were running that is! The service was not that good and missing the last bus home meant a long walk through deserted building sites, with the odd built up area on the way. The other means of transport was the "bonde," similar to San Francisco's famous tramcars. Those who could not afford the ticket, hung off the back, ready to jump off if an inspector came along.

Despite the difficulties of getting there, Interlagos was the only race track in the whole country worthy of the name. Even the great Fangio, who had just taken his fifth world championship title at the time, had shone there, winning a Sports Car race in a Maserati 300 S on 1st December 1957. Rio also had a circuit at Boa Vista, where Fangio took another win after the one at Interlagos. Later, Brasilia would boast a race track where Emerson Fittipaldi won a non-championship Formula 1 race in 1974.

Until Fittipaldi appeared on the scene, Brazilian racing stars had been few and far between at international level. In Formula 1, Chico Landi, had competed in six grands prix for Ferrari and Maserati between 1951 and 1956. Over the same period, Hermano Da Silva Ramos, no relation to Ayrton and a Franco-Brazilian who lived in Paris, had raced in Formula 1 and 2, as well as sports cars, mainly for Gordini. A Renault dealer, Bino Heinz, had raced a bit in sports cars, mainly at Sebring in a Maserati. Having taken on an Alpine dealership, he took part in the 1963 Le Mans 24 Hours in a prototype built by the French company, but he was killed racing. It was hardly a career to inspire others. In any case, the number one sport in Brazil was of course football, both in terms of popularity and the number of those taking part. "King Pele" was a national hero. Until Emerson Fittipaldi, like Ayrton a Paulista, became World Champion, no one could believe that one day, the whole country would be passionate about Formula 1. Ayrton was only twelve then and fourteen when Fittipaldi took his second title. "Emo" was totally unaware of his young compatriot, who was then a rising star in the world of karting and of the fact that Senna would one day eclipse him in terms of glory both at home and indeed on the world stage. In the meantime, everything was set for what would be the irresistible rise of Ayrton Senna da Silva. ■

• **1 and 2**_The most important thing in Ayrton's life was always his family. On the left, with his mother Neide and his younger brother Leonardo, in the days before he before he became a global star. On the right, with his father Milton, a frequent visitor to the tracks to keep an eye on his son. Not forgetting his sister Viviane with whom he worked for charity in the later stages of his career.

Chapter 2
Interlagos

At the start of the Sixties, the da Silva family was well established in the sprawling city of São Paulo and was comfortably well off. They did not live in the opulent and arrogant splendour of a small and favoured elite, but their situation was secure thanks to determination and hard work. The house was comfortable and admittedly a "palace" by the standards of those who lived in the favelas, but it was a "shack" to those nabobs sitting on their colossal fortunes. Married to Neide Joanna Senna, Milton Guirado da Silva started on the bottom rung of the ladder and was a self-made man. From relatively poor beginnings he started off by driving...other people. He was a chauffeur. Then, he set up a small automobile spare parts business, which began to flourish at the end of the Fifties. He was a man with strict moral values and his feet firmly on the ground. For him, getting rich was not a goal in itself. Achieving wealth took hard work and there was no room for daydreaming. Nevertheless, he was very proud of the fact that his family was well provided for, but he would be less demanding when it came to providing his nearest and dearest with the wherewithal to indulge the objects of their passing whims. Later, he diversified, making several astute and profitable investments. He bought land and livestock, creating an agricultural establishment. By the time Ayrton was a global sports star, he too got involved in expanding the property which now counted more than 10,000 head of cattle and around 400,000 hectares of land. By then the da Silva family had joined the very small clique of the extremely wealthy and Milton was able to oversee his operation in his own private plane.

Milton and Neide had three children: a daughter Viviane in 1957, then two sons, Ayrton in 1960 and Leonardo in 1966. Neide came from a Brazilian middle class background and spent all her time looking after her children and she was very close to all of them. Viviane recalled that the young Ayrton was a bundle of energy, which often led to cuts and bruises, which worried his mother, who always wanted to pack him off to the doctor! He simply needed an outlet for his energies and it was his father who found it for him, noting Ayrton's interest in the dashboard of the family car, as he mimicked every action required to keep a car in motion. Milton da Silva was interested in motorised sports and gave his lad a little Jeep pedal-car, then more significantly, a kart with a real little engine which backfired and brakes which just about slowed it down. Ayrton was only four at the time.

In 1964, karting was still in its infancy and not well established in the public's imagination. In the Fifties, American flyers with little to do at their airfields in between missions, made little chassis out of welded tubes, to which they fitted lawn mower engines. Known as "go-karts," they grew in popularity in the Sixties and soon developed their own niche in the pantheon of motor sports. It was still a long way off the serious sport it is today and it was generally regarded as an amusing pastime for the well-heeled. 1964 was the decisive year when karting became established at a higher level with the creation of a world championship, won that year by Italy's Guido Sala. Races grew with bigger grids and the calendar expanded as the equipment also became more professional. However, no one could predict for a moment that these little machines with their lively and rapid performance would one day be seen as a breeding ground for the best drivers in the world, who would go on to drive the most powerful cars. Karting champions were still restricted to their own entertaining and convivial little world. It was only a decade later that the cream would rise to the top with names like Riccardo Patrese and Eddie Cheever and eventually, virtually the entire Formula 1 grid of the Eighties and Nineties, including Ayrton Senna of course.

As far as Milton was concerned, the gift of the little kart was nothing more than a way of channelling his kid's energies in a direction to which he already seemed drawn. Indeed, Ayrton would spend many a happy hour dashing down the slope alongside the family home, braking hard before turning round and heading once again for the top, before starting all over again. As the child got older and went to school, the rules of engagement were outlined by the father: okay for the karting, but like all rewards it had to be worked for. Ayrton's report cards would decide.

During his entire time at school, Ayrton Senna never shone in the classroom. Generally impatient, homework would usually be consigned to the last ten minutes before going out. Intelligent and intuitive, he always knew how to get away with the minimum asked for, to avoid getting into any annoying bother, such as not being allowed to drive his kart for example.

In 1970, the boy started at the Colegio Rio Branco, a strict and spartan private school, where, according to the recollections of his teachers, who liked him nevertheless, he acquitted himself no better than he had done in the past. He was a nice boy, not without charm. But his mind was on other things. That first kart no longer satisfied his needs. He had dismantled it dozens of times, analysing the engine and its performance and explained to his puzzled father that he needed something more powerful! As his school work was more or less to the required standard, Milton gave in. Fitted with an engine which matched his aspirations, Ayrton spent every moment of his free time charging round the tarmac at the Interlagos kart track, which was only three quarters of an

hour away from his home. The track was not far from the circuit which would soon be home to the Formula 1 Grand Prix. It was pretty basic, as were all kart tracks of that era. Nevertheless, it boasted concrete pits with corrugated iron roofs and even, unusual for the time, a small grandstand. In the afternoon, after school and at the weekends, the kid's time was devoted to this all-consuming passion, even if he still had a bit of time for building model airplanes and playing table-tennis. The young adolescent engaged in a tireless quest for performance and made sure he was fully au fait with the mechanical side. According to those who knew him at the time, he already knew everything about braking. He never stopped dismantling the calipers and the little disc, while fine tuning the movement of the brake pedal. With several engines and carburettors, he tried every single permutation, comparing compression ratios and the jets in the carburettors. He would never settle for less than perfection. It rains often in São Paulo and, at first, he was not particularly skilled in these conditions. Wanting to learn and understand, Ayrton

● **3**_While the mechanics work on the engine, the young driver is all concentration as he mentally prepares for the race.

SIPA Presse

therefore took the decision that every time the heavens opened, he would get out his kart and would run for hours in the rain, until dusk brought him to a halt when he could no longer see his feet in front of him. This total commitment to mastering a subject which he felt eluded him would crop up again on numerous occasions and would be one of the building blocks of his later career as a legendary driver. Senna was already showing himself to be relentless in his pursuit of a solution to whatever problem stood in his way. Nothing could be left to chance and no detail of engine tuning or chassis set-up could be ignored. It certainly delighted and staggered in equal measure the rotund man with a luxuriant moustache who watched with fascination from the pits. Lucio Pascual Gascon, known as "Tche" knew he had a customer who was out of the ordinary.

Once Milton da Silva realised that his son could only talk of nuts and bolts, he realised that this talent, if that's what it really was, had to be exploited correctly. As a pragmatic man and an attentive father, he wanted his son to succeed, but with the best chance possible. He seemed to realise that Ayrton spent more time with the people in the street and at the circuit, than with the sons of good families from the Colegio Rio Branco. He realised quiet rightly, that if he was going to get involved in some sort of project, then it might as well be with the right person. So he made his own discrete enquiries about racing and how to find the ideal mechanic to prepare and run the kart. His enquiries came up with the name of "Tche," whom he contacted immediately about looking after his son. Originally Spanish, Gascon had come to Brazil twenty five years earlier and was the top man in local karting circles, whose school had seen the likes of Fittipaldi and Pace pass through its doors. It was now June 1973, when these two names had gained heroic status at home. Carlos Pace made his Formula 1 debut with the Surtees team, while Emerson Fittipaldi was a living god! World Champion in 1972 at the wheel of the superb black and gold JPS Lotus 72, he won the first official Formula 1 Grand Prix to be staged at Interlagos. Indeed, Milton was there in the paddock, with his son Ayrton, who was presented to the great champion, who actually seemed to take an interest in what the little chap was doing in karting. From then on, Emerson always kept an experienced eye on Senna's career and was there for him in the difficult moments. He was also there twenty one years later to accompany Ayrton, now himself a god for an entire nation, on his last journey to his final resting place at the Morumbi cemetery.

From the very beginning, Tche would be a privileged witness to the fantastic ascent of the young Paulista. On 1st July 1973, Ayrton da Silva (this being the family name under which he raced for some time) was at the Interlagos karting track, with his chassis number 42. He had been there since six in the morning to be sure of leaving nothing to chance! Having taken part in several friendly races, this was his first official event, as Brazilian law forbade drivers to compete under the age of thirteen. He dominated the event and took the chequered flag, waved of course by Tche himself. Lucio Pascual Gascon took several days to think about it, but made up his mind: he wanted to look after and train this little marvel and said "yes" to Milton da Silva. There would be total complicity between this rough and ready Spaniard and the skinny Brazilian for the next three years and their friendship never waned. Ayrton read the specialist magazines, the results from Europe and learnt about the performance of the various engines and chassis, ordering the best to be sent to Brazil. Tche did the preparation, always watched by this attentive and punctilious kid. Armed with a driver and a truck, transformed into a mobile workshop, provided by Papa da Silva, the two of them travelled the country competing in ever more important races. With every passing day, Ayrton revealed more and more skill at the wheel and spent ages discussing technical matters with his mentor, who never tired of listening to the young virtuoso and his precise way of explaining what he did and didn't want!

At the start of 1974, Ayrton da Silva won the important title of Champion of São Paulo in the junior category, and the following year he was runner-up in the Brazilian series. In 1976, he moved up to the 100 cc category, but despite some good finishes, did not take any wins. However, his controlled sliding technique was drawing more and more admirers. Maurizio Sandro Sala was only moderately impressed by the Paulista. A few years older, he had forged a solid reputation as one of the hard men of the pack and he had no plans to abdicate to this young phenomenon, who had become the darling of the crowds. For his part, Ayrton was galvanised by the fact he was in the lead and going quickly. This motivation would last him all the way through into his Formula 1 days. He had no time to fight in the pack, he wanted to be out in front with everyone else behind him. There were the inevitable collisions, but Ayrton would often pass the great Maurizio. At the end of 1976, Sala left Brazil for England and single-seaters and Ayrton da Silva decided, in consultation with Tche and his father, to go for the Inter category, the International South American championship. ∎

Roberto Piccinini Archives

Chapter 3
Inter...
Nacional Ayrton

DPPI/Froissart

The inter category is vitally important for any
young karting ace. It's like stepping into the
big kid's playground, the final stage before...
before what in fact? What does one do when
one has won everything in karts and one is too
old to fend off the young chargers coming up
from behind? Ayrton did not seem to ask himself
that question. All his energies were directed at
one day becoming karting world champion.
When they met at a race track, Chico Serra spoke
to him about car racing, having spent a summer
in England, but it did not really grab his
attention. Serra was three years older than
Ayrton and therefore more experienced. He was
particularly up on all the little tricks of the trade
like brake testing someone stuck up your exhaust
pipe going down the straight just to unnerve
them. He tried it with Ayrton but, aware of these
tricks, the youngster made the most of the
moment to nip by and win the race. Apart from
their confrontations on the track, they got on
fine, as the elder Chico would be one step ahead
of Ayrton everywhere, be it in Formula Ford or
Formula 1, the only difference being their
different track records.

In 1977, Ayrton contested the classic
national events in his new category, instantly

racking up good results. In fact, these races were
mere rehearsals for the main event which took
place in San Jose in Uruguay. He left Brazil for
the first time. It was an important step, as the
South American championship represented the
first step towards global recognition. It was a
high class entry, even if it was not a patch on
what could be found in Europe, but Ayrton was
not concerned about that. He dominated the
event, eventually walking off with the coveted
title. From now on, he was on the road to success
which would lead to the great wide world. This
title was actually no more than a stepping stone
to the supreme crown of world champion, to
which he would devote himself for the next
three years. It would be the only title to elude
him.

Aware of the fact that the karting elite and
the professionals were all in Europe, Ayrton did
not need convincing to accept an offer from the
Brazilian federation to head for the Old
Continent along with the country's other top
drivers, to the 1978 world championship, held at
Le Mans. But this would require better
equipment and, at the time, the Italians were
noted for their expertise in this area. Milto da
Silva contacted the Parilla brothers, who ran the

D.A.P. (Di Angelo Parilla) firm named after their father who invented the famous rotary valve on two-stroke engines, still the ultimate in international karting. Honoured to be approached by the family of the South American champion, as Ayrton had just won that year's Inter title in Brazil, Achille and Angelo Parilla reached an agreement with Milton, to test the equipment in Italy, prior to the world championship. Arriving for the first time in Europe, Ayrton da Silva was taken to the Parma-Pancrazio circuit and met up with the Italian team and their machines.

Right from his very first laps, it was obvious to all the observers that they were watching something a bit special. His driving style impressed and soon the young maestro's times showed the true story. Ayrton was already lapping as quickly as the works driver, Ireland's Terry Fullerton, who was there as an incredulous witness. Fullerton was not just anybody: he was world champion in 1973 and, despite his advancing years – he was 28! – he was also there to prepare for the world championships. Totally convinced by this first demonstration, the Parilla brothers offered Ayrton a works contract, as

• **6**_Ayrton da Silva poses for the traditional driver presentation at Le Mans prior to the 1978 World Championship. The fans finally get to see the young face hidden underneath the yellow helmet, who had been so impressive in qualifying.

number 2 to Fullerton. He would not be paid, but he would get the best equipment he had ever used. Ayrton then spent two weeks testing intensively, going through the chassis, engines and tyres. It was a laborious task, but vital in that finding the best engine from a batch and the right tyres is an empirical science and only the very best drivers have sufficient feeling to sense any hesitation in an engine or carburettor. Competition between these future champions is extremely close with places on a karting grid often split by just thousandths of a second.

Testing late into the night was a great way for a driver to get the hang of what was involved.

The big day arrived: Ayrton met up with his fellow countrymen on 11th September 1978 in the Le Mans paddock, with its karting track inside the 24 Hours circuit. He was also delighted to find Tche, who had made the trip to support his young charger. Let go by Milton, Pascual Gascon no longer had a technical role in the operation, but he was there to act as a reassuring translator for the young man whose command of Italian was not yet good enough to converse with the

DPPI/ Froissart

• **7**_Checking the weaponry at the world championships in Nivelles in 1980. Ayrton in that characteristic reflective pose which would typify him throughout his career.

DPPI/ Froissart

Italian mechanics from D.A.P. For the European spectators, it was their first sighting of the yellow helmet with green and blue stripes, as it whizzed around the track. He only just missed out on pole, which went to Fullerton, but he had made his mark and his excellent showing in the pre-finals meant that he was immediately considered a favourite for the main event. Unfortunately, a collision due to a lack of experience ruined any hopes of victory and he finished sixth.

It was a flattering result for a first attempt, but of course Ayrton was not happy with it. He wanted to win and swore he would do it one day. Serra spoke to him again about car racing, saying he should try his luck in England. But at the time, Senna did not want to dilute his efforts and added that he was not really interested in the car thing. It was certainly true, but one could surmise that he had other secret thoughts on his mind which he did not want to divulge until the situation was clear.

He knew that all this, the karts, the racing, would soon have to end. It was a family rule that work takes precedence. He was the eldest of the Senna da Silva sons and as such, at some point, he would have to take over from Milton. The father had never thought otherwise and he regarded the karting merely as a hobby. He had

encouraged his son, believing that high level competition was character building and would help when it came to running a large company like his. But once the world championship had been reached and the follies of youth had passed, it would be time to think of getting back to the real world. That was pretty much Milton da Silva's line of thought and Ayrton was well aware of it.

Despite this, the young champion dispensed all his energies and means to be as ready as possible for the 1979 world championship. He went back to Brazil and, apart from a few haphazard courses in business studies at the University of Sao Paolo, he spent almost all his time at improving and testing, all possible permutations of chassis and engine, under the watchful eye of Tche. Having competed in the major South American races, Ayrton flew to Portugal in September to the little seaside town of Estoril, which was hosting the world championship.

Unlike the previous year at Le Mans, this time he turned up at the race track as the favourite. The D.A.P. team was made up of the ever-present Terry Fullerton and a new driver, Dutchman Peter Koene, the Dutch importer for the Italian factory. Despite a coming together with Fullerton in qualifying, Ayrton did an

● **8**_In a class of his own at Nivelles. Senna, now wearing a yellow helmet with green and blue bands, eclipsed everyone in qualifying. But, come race day, an unfortunate collision lost him any chance of becoming world champion.

excellent time and his biggest threat now appeared to come from Koene. The start of the final was the scene of much confusion, which was down to the organisers and tensions grew on the grid as the time ticked by. Ayrton da Silva did not flinch, did not speak. He stayed in his kart, concentrating hard on what had to be the race of his life. It was an attitude which would be noted time and again later in his single-seater career, reflecting the ability to cut himself off from the outside world, something rarely seen in his contemporaries at the time. The pack was finally released and the yellow helmet gradually disappeared into the distance, as Ayrton thrilled the crowd with his unique style, often sliding for long distances, sometimes steering with just one hand, while the other fiddled with the carburettor. For the Portuguese fans, this "cousin" of theirs was a real phenomenon who was bound to win. Despite a closing pack, Ayrton reigned supreme and led as he pleased. The laps ticked by and eventually he was shown the number "1" as he passed in front of the signalling area. Only one lap between him and total happiness. Another 1100 metres and he would take the

chequered flag, arms held aloft as he received a tumultuous ovation. He is world champion!

But as dusk fell on the circuit, the drivers stepped up onto the podium: a beaming Peter Koene jumped onto the top step and a sulking Ayrton da Silva was only second! In those days, the final result was based on the classification of the three finals: with Ayrton and Peter on level pegging, the performance in qualifying was taken into account and in this instance, the Dutchman had done better. Ayrton could not cope with this mathematical solution. He won on the track and could not deal with the injustice of it all. He would never admit it and it would remain one of the two biggest disappointments of his career; the other being his second place in the 1984 Formula 1 Monaco Grand Prix.

His obsession with being the best in the world would relegate everything else to second place. In 1980 the fact he was champion of both Brazil and South America brought him little satisfaction for just a short space of time. There was nothing new to savour in that and it was just a rehearsal for the final confrontation. This time it took place in Belgium, at the Nivelles-Baulers circuit, where six years earlier, Riccardo Patrese,

Eyewitness account of Marc Boulineau

Marc Boulineau came late to karting, at an age when professional drivers are already at their peak. He was 25 when he tackled international competition in the Seventies. A purely amateur racer, he raced without factory support. Nevertheless, he won several national titles and his prowess took him to third place in the 1983 world championships at Le Mans. He therefore had the pleasure of meeting a certain Ayrton Da Silva on the European circuits:

"I came across him at Le Mans in '78. It was our first sighting of Senna da Silva and he had been sensational in qualifying. He had an attacking nature which had rarely been seen in karting. He attacked even when there was no room. It was surprising and you could see him passing other drivers with two wheels on the track and the other two on the kerb. He therefore got ahead of drivers who thought they hadn't left him any room! I had little contact with him. He was quite introverted. I think he was a 100% absorbed by racing. From the outside, he was someone who did not joke much with the other drivers. I remember when he was with the Parilla brothers and they worked well together because they were also a bit insular. Work and qualifying did not frighten them. I was sometimes in the next door pits and he worked a lot on his settings, more than the other drivers that's for sure. He had factory backing and he could have settled for good lap times, but no. Even if he was quickest, he wanted to beat his own time and go quicker still.
He was a very quick driver, very talented, but he did not know how to wait. I saw him at Jesolo one year when he had some spectacular crashes, particularly after colliding with Wilson. In F1, he had similar incidents, but well, he was still one of the greats."

Eyewitness account of Lionel Froissart

A journalist who covered, amongst other things, Formula 1 for the French daily "Liberation" since 1986, Lionel Froissart started in 1978, logically one could say, with karting. It was during that year's world championship at Le Mans, that he first came across Ayrton Senna:

"*Unlike the others, he was sliding a long way before the corner, until he found grip. The tyres were really improving at this time and he was on the limit on two wheels. On some tracks, he made the most of this ability to run on two wheels to cut corners without hammering his kart on the kerbs. He didn't do it all the time; it depended on the tracks, but he was always sliding. Maybe he would do it less today, now that the tyres have evolved. He was very skilful and could do several things at once, such as using his right hand to adjust the mixture screw on his carburettor while steering with his left hand. He adapted to the circuit, the engine characteristics, the temperature and the tyres. He could play with his settings, which others could not do. The usual procedure was to make one setting and maybe change it towards the end of the race if things were really bad. He would also start with his right hand on the carburettor for the first few metres, then he would take his hand off, releasing a huge cloud of smoke. It was the D.A.P. engine which required this technique. It certainly added to the spectacle.*"

• **9**_In the 1981 world championship at Parma-Pancrazio, Ayrton struggled with inferior equipment when it came to fighting on the track.

Roberto Piccinini Archives

● **10**_On the Parma track, stars of the future go head to head: Ayrton Senna (no. 9) leads Ivan Capelli (no. 27).

by now an Arrows Formula 1 driver, had taken the title. This year, Ayrton would cross swords with another Dutchman, Peter de Bruyn and of course, his old adversary, Terry Fullerton. In qualifying, there was little to chose between them and each man then concentrated on preparing his weapon for the final. Shortly after the start, Ayrton was knocked off the track by another driver, clumsy or conniving, depending on your point of view. Once back on track, the Brazilian went flat out to make up for lost time, but he had to face the facts: his engine was under too much strain and losing power and all hope was gone. De Bruyn crossed the line to win and Ayrton was second yet again. As for Fullerton, he too had been knocked out of the race and almost came to blows with the guilty party.

In 1981, the International Karting Commission modified the technical regulations for the top drivers, creating a new K class, based on 135 cc engines. The small constructors, like D.A.P. did not have the means to continue. World karting was becoming more professional as it matured. That year, Ayrton Senna da Silva had also taken a step forward and was now racing single-seaters in the British Formula Ford championship. But the unsatiated desire to pick up that wretched kart title which had always snubbed him, led him to accept an offer for one more go at it with the Parilla brothers. This year the world championship would be held at the Parma track where he had his first test. The young man was faithful to his friendships and the relationship which tied him to Achille and Angelo was more than purely professional. He knew what he owed them and he decided to

throw in his lot with them, come what may. The equipment put at his disposal, with 127 cc engines, meant that Ayrton could not fight for the lead. Despite his talent and his pugnacity, he did no better than fourth at the Parma track, even though he knew it so well. The winner Mike Wilson went on to stamp his authority on the event, winning six titles between 1981 and 1989. Ayrton never lost his admiration for the Italian's prowess and told him so himself, when they met in 1993 for the Masters of Karting in Paris-Bercy.

In 1982, he was talked into it once again and headed off to Sweden with D.A.P. At the Kalmar circuit, the reality of the situation finally dawned on him. This time there was no hope given that his equipment was really obsolete. Qualifying was a disaster because of a technical problem which relegated him to 60th place. His natural talent took over in the race and he made a charge for glory before a collision and the inevitable retirement. It was over. Ayrton realised at last that he would never be karting world champion. However, his professional life had taken a definitive turn towards car racing, but ending this chapter of his youth with a failure made him uneasy. He then headed off to Porto Alegre for the Brazilian championship which he won for a final time. When he became a Formula 1 champion, he built a kart track of his own at his Tatui home, acquired in 1988, situated in the countryside to the north east of Sao Paolo. There he rediscovered the fun of these little machines, which he shared with his nephew Bruno, son of Viviane and he also organised a few friendly races prior to the Brazilian Grand Prix. ■

● **11**_At the Race of Champions at Jesolo in 1981, spectacular crashes, especially the one between Ayrton Senna and Mike Wilson, would decide the outcome of the race. The Brazilian is already looking to single-seaters and knows that karting is (almost) over.

Chapter 4
The big decision

• 12_The South American rivals: the old hands, Alfonso Toledano (on left) and Enrique Mansilla (on right) gather round the new-boy, Ayrton da Silva. Note Ayrton's immaculate race overalls which belie his tight racing budget.

After failing at Nivelles in 1980, Ayrton Senna da Silva's thoughts turned once again to what Chico Serra, now in his second year in England, had told him. The changes to the karting regulations did not hold the promise of much and in fact, car racing actually appealed more than he would admit to. He got in touch with Chico and asked him to talk to Ralf Firman on his behalf. Firman was the boss of the Van Diemen company whose cars made up half the field in Formula Ford 1600 at the time, including Serra in 1977. The Brazilian did such a good PR job on his young compatriot that Firman agreed to give Senna a test. Ayrton still had to convince his parents, especially his father. Milton agreed with apparent good grace, seeing this foreign sojourn as a character building

experience. He even financed half a season for his son, the other half more or less taken care of by Ralf Firman himself. But this time, the terms were clear and at the end of the season, Ayrton was to return to study economics at university and would give up motor racing for ever. Ayrton accepted the "contract." He still had to convince one more person whose approval he definitely needed.

Ayrton Senna da Silva had just married Liliane Vasconcelos de Souza. She no doubt imagined a straightforward life in São Paulo with a husband who ran a company and lived a contented family life. As far as she was concerned, his departure for England was a necessary rite of passage in Ayrton's life, which she hoped would be as short as possible. The young couple therefore landed at Heathrow in February 1981 in the damp and cold of a British winter. It was a depressing arrival, brightened up by the presence of Chico Serra who put them up for a while, before he rented a small apartment near Snetterton circuit in Norfolk. It was at this track that Ayrton had his first encounter with his Van Diemen. In fact, it was just a test to sort out driver position and other adjustments and the new car which he had ordered would not arrive until the start of March for the second race on his programme.

The young Brazilian had arranged to tackle two championships: the Townsend-Thoresen and the RAC. But he started his car racing career in a P&O Ferries race on 1st March at Brands Hatch. His car was not ready yet and so he drove a year old model with a less than competitive engine. The P&O series was of no interest to him in terms of points, but it provided an excellent opportunity to discover the hectic nature of the English grids, especially as a barely tolerated

foreigner. History records on the entry list that Van Diemen RF 80 no. 6 was driven by a certain "Ayerton de Silva." On the results sheet, his first name had been correctly spelt and no one would ever get the name Ayrton da Silva wrong again, as they all knew who he was!

He finished fifth at the end of a steady race, learning a lot along the way. The Formula Ford 1600 was a simple beast, with no wings, narrow grooved tyres, minimal aerodynamics and an uncomplicated engine. It needed a firm hand on the wheel and offered drivers the chance to learn the ropes of racing itself, before having to get the hang of setting up a car. He also got to meet his main opposition; the Englishman Rick Morris, the Mexican Alfonso Toledano and the Argentine Enrique Mansilla, who came first that day. The two foreigners were old hands and regarded as favourites for the season by the pundits. For Ayrton, they simply represented rivals who were there to be beaten. The following Sunday at Thruxton, Ayrton finally got his hands on his own car, a Van Diemen RF 81-Minister,

● **13**_Earlier smiles make way for aggression on track. At Snetterton, da Silva (no. 4) is the meat in a sandwich between Toledano (no. 1) and Mansilla (no. 3.) The young Brazilian would soon eclipse all his rivals. Behind them are Rick Morris, Steve Lincoln and Andy Ackerley.

painted yellow and black. He finished third. Then the circus moved to Brands Hatch on 15th March for a rainy weekend. The wet track meant that each driver had his own idea of the ideal way to tackle the corners. After a good practice session, Ayrton started from the front row, between poleman Morris and another English driver, Andy Ackerley, who passed the Brazilian round the outside at Paddock Bend. But as he headed down the straight to Druids hairpin, he saw the yellow and black Van Diemen dive down the inside. Ackerley tried to close the door, but Senna stuck to his guns, the two cars touched and poor Ackerley's race ended there in the gravel. Ayrton was never worried again and lead all 15 laps of the final. He had just started a series of wins which his rivals and the spectators would remember for a long time.

He then embarked on a programme of 17 races, spread over two championships running up to September. He finished just once in fourth place at Brands Hatch on 12th July, when a water pipe broke. In all the others, Ayrton da Silva was on the podium: 12 wins, including the first one just described and five second places! He was totally dominant. Not only did he take both titles, but his rivals were now completely demoralised. With Ayrton, it seemed the rules of track craft had been rewritten. His lines could be unbelievable, especially in the rain, but he would always take the lead. The Paulista had learnt all about aggressive behaviour in the pack and his racing experience increased immeasurably. He had more than lived up to expectations and on top of that, he was beginning to carve out a reputation, earning the recognition of pundits

• **14**_Ayrton da Silva goes round the outside of an opponent, in the rain at Brands Hatch, demonstrating a style that would soon become legendary.

and those in the sport. One of those was Dennis Rushen, who ran the Rushen Green Racing Formula Ford 2000 team. He was convinced of Senna's talent after seeing him in action at Snetterton on Sunday 9th August and immediately offered him a works drive for 1982, with a good salary. Never one to rush into things, Ayrton took the offer on board with a polite thank you and asked for time to think about it. Contrary to appearances, Ayrton's life was getting more and more difficult.

Liliane had had enough. Their life together was a failure and they hardly saw one another. How could she share her life with a man whose days were filled with racing cars and racing? Ayrton found the situation very hard to deal with. He spent his days at the factory, talking shop, overseeing the build process and checking the car set-up. Just as he did in his karting days, he spent all his time concentrating on the work which would become his future. He did not want to leave anything to chance. He had to understand everything, down to the smallest detail. Anything else was of secondary importance. Anything else obviously included Liliane, but there was no apparent solution. In

mid-September, the couple flew to Parma, where Ayrton was taking part in the karting world championship. He met up with people he was close to: the Parilla brothers, his parents, the D.A.P. mechanics and this little break in the Italian sunshine, in the middle of his hectic schedule, definitely helped him to see things more clearly. He spoke to his father Milton about the future. Back in England for the 13th round of the Townsend-Thoresen Championship at Brands Hatch on 29th September, he finished second to make sure of the title before the season was over. When asked by a journalist what his plans were for 1982, he said he would not be back.

Ayrton had made a decision and explained to an incredulous press that he wanted to live in Brazil. Racing only interested him if he enjoyed it and the idea of having to find sponsors for an international programme did not appeal to him. He would take over the running of a small business, with help from his father and would only take part in the odd kart race for the fun of it. He then called Ralph Firman to tell him he would not be completing his race programme and that he was flying back to South America. Liliane was smiling again.

● **15**_In 1981, the opposition was powerless against the incredible determination of the Brazilian. Here, Robert Gibbs cracks under pressure from the now much feared yellow and black Van Diemen.

From October 1981 to February 1982, Ayrton Senna settled into his new life, invigorated by being back with his family and the warm weather. A tropical summer was in prospect and the future company boss finally passed his economics exams. Milton, a strict but nevertheless attentive father, observed his son go through this new phase in his life. He had done all in his power to make Ayrton happy but he felt the boy was melancholy and distant. So when, Ayrton called together the family for a meeting at the start of 1982, Milton already knew what was coming. The young man had done all he could to convince himself that Brazil was where his future lay. But, ever since that interview with the British press in September 1981 he had been lying to himself and to those around him. He no longer wished to continue with a life that did not suit him. He spoke of his real motivation, of racing and of an overwhelming need to continue, to go further and higher. He wanted to become the best in what he thought he was good at. He had to return to England.

Milton agreed. Ayrton would race again, but as a professional this time. His father found him a business adviser, who was an old family friend, Armando Botelho Teixeira. He had already looked after the kid's minor contracts in his karting days and now his job was to negotiate at a much higher level. They worked together all the way up to Formula 1, until the death of Teixeira in 1989. Armando set up a promotions company in São Paulo, run by a cousin of the da Silvas, Fabio da Silva Machado. Ayrton immediately got in touch again with Dennis Rushen and accepted the offer the team boss had made him at Snetterton back in August 1981: £10,000 for a season in Formula Ford 2000. He actually turned down an offer from Murray Taylor to jump straight into Formula 3, preferring to make progress one step at a time rather than rush things. The programme was packed: 28 races spread across the British championship, the Pace British FF2000 and the European series, run by the European Formula Drivers' Association. The main aim of course was to make it at international level, to learn the circuits and to get noticed. As four of the events were curtain raisers to Formula 1 Grands Prix, they presented an opportunity to make some important contacts. In March 1982, he rediscovered England, its climate and its races. His rented apartment was just somewhere to sleep as he was totally immersed in his race programme. As always, he wanted the odds to be stacked in his favour and his work methods had not changed and would never change in fact. He was a stickler for detail and would stun everyone with his obsessional desire to master every aspect of his work. Immersing himself totally in the job also served the additional purpose of combating the homesickness he felt whenever his mind wandered back across the Atlantic and his thoughts turned to his family, the sunshine and the country air. Maybe he also thought of Liliane, who had asked him for a divorce. ∎

● **16**_"Let's get ourselves organised!" At the request of Milton da Silva, Armando Botelho Teixeira took over the running of the young Senna's career from 1982, in order to tackle the new season and future ones in a professional manner.

Chapter 5
The birth of Ayrton Senna

● **17**_The FF2000 had more sophisticated aerodynamics than the FF1600 and required some learning. No problem for Ayrton Senna, seen here in attacking mode at Oulton Park on 27th March 1982 in the second round of the English championship. He put together all the necessary elements to crucify the opposition.

The Formula Ford 2000 differed from his previous mount essentially in having a 2 litre engine. But in 1982, there was a novelty for the competitors in this class: for the first time, the cars were fitted with a rear wing, two front wing elements and slick tyres. The changes altered the way they needed to be driven with a lot more set-up permutations, which provided good training for young drivers hoping for glory in the higher formulae. Ayrton was once again in a Van Diemen, an RF82, as the Rushen Green Racing team was linked in with Ralf Firman. Once again, it was painted yellow and black with the name Ayrton Senna written on its sides, even though the entry list still spoke of da Silva. As if to mark the change of philosophy which this

return to England entailed, Ayrton decided to dump the da Silva, which was very common in Brazil, adopting his mother's family name, Senna. The subtext was that it was also a subconscious way of cutting the paternal ties and taking charge of his own destiny. For their part, the team mechanics, who could not cope with the sing-song diphthongs of the Brazilian language, decided to call him...Harry!

While reeling off a load of statistics can be tedious, it is fascinating to see to what extent "Harry" destroyed the opposition in 1982. In the British championship, he won 16 out of 19 races, or out of 18 if one allows for the fact that he missed the Oulton Park race at the end of May, because of tyre problems. In the EFDA series, he won 6 times out of 9, retiring 3 times. Taking the season as a whole, he was only beaten fair and square on two occasions, one of them in the British Championship, when Ayrton had already won the title and lacked enthusiasm for proceedings. Finally, a figure which signalled what would become a speciality of his, he took 13 poles in England and nothing less than all of them in the European races! Naturally, he picked up both titles as he pleased and this fantastic wave of success opened several doors at the end of the year, including an invitation to drive in a Formula 3 race, which he won.

Those who observed the progress of the yellow and black Van Diemen through the year noticed that there was an evolution in the way Senna was cornering, with a purer line through the corners and a more refined turn of speed. The reason was simple: the slick tyres could not be tortured in the way the grooved ones could on the FF 1600 and Ayrton had learnt that lesson very quickly. His technical feeling for a car was progressing at an incredible rate. His chief mechanic, a Swede by the name of Peter Dahl, recalls that in the space of two short laps, Ayrton

was capable of spotting a less than perfect tyre in a set, asking for it to be changed. His concentration was all consuming over a race weekend and already, at this stage in his career, he refused to be distracted from his work, which gave him an image that would stick with him for a long time; that of a man who never laughed. But Dennis Rushen maintains he was perfectly normal and liked to have fun with his mates. Although the moment he got to the track, he put himself under pressure and it was best not to rile him. His friends came mainly from among his fellow Brazilian exiles: Chico Serra, older than him and Mauricio Gugelmin, younger by three years, with whom he shared a flat in Reading and who made it into Formula 1 in the late Eighties, for a short and frustrating career. Driving in Formula Ford 1600, Mauricio was a first hand witness of one of his fellow countryman's greatest exploits during the year. It was a cornerstone on which to build a legend.

It took place at Snetterton on 9th April, at the sixth round of the British championship. Just seeing the name Ayrton Senna written on an entry list was enough to put the wind up the

● **18**_One of the great moments of the 1982 championship: At Snetterton on 9th April, Calvin Fish (no. 74) had thought he had finally got the better of the Brazilian whirlwind. But having fixed his brake problem, Senna staged a memorable fight back, leaving poor Fish for dead.

other competitors. The Brazilian phenomenon had won the first five rounds, setting pole and fastest race lap each time! England's Calvin Fish was best placed to cross swords with Senna, but was beginning to ask himself if this damned yellow helmet hid any possible weakness. That day on the Norfolk track, he thought he had finally found one. Inexplicably, the leading Van Diemen slowed and the Englishman was able to savour the joy of overtaking and for once could forget the terror of the track, or so he thought. A few laps later, he had to cope with the sight of the yellow and black car gradually growing in size in his mirrors. Ayrton overtook in his incomparable fashion and went on to win. Speaking to Gugelmin, who was waiting for him at the finish, Senna laughed that he only had rear brakes. He had suddenly felt the pedal go long as the front brakes had gone, thanks to a stone which had cut through a brake line. He instantly switched the brake balance 100% to the rear, while slackening off the roll bar. He took a few laps to get used to the different handling of the car, which allowed Calvin Fish and Russell Spence to get by. With all his brakes at the rear, the car felt to Senna like something from his karting days and once he was comfortable with the new set-up, he closed the gap in a handful

of laps and retook the lead as though nothing had happened. At the end of the story, Gugelmin was not convinced and touched the front discs. They were stone cold!

The 1982 series in England was a complete nightmare for all his opponents. Only Frank Bradley and Calvin Fish managed to beat the incredible Brazilian: the former at Snetterton on 4th July, when he was the only driver to have stayed out on slicks on a wet track which dried out completely. Senna was very complimentary in fact about this great gamble. The latter did it at the final round at Brands Hatch, when the championship had already been decided in Ayrton's favour. With 16 wins, 2 seconds and one DNS, the young Paulista had literally sickened his opponents and made his mark.

While the European EFDA series eventually ended in the best way possible, it got off to a frustrating start for Ayrton. Pumped up by his fantastic debut in the British series, he did not cope well with a broken engine in the first leg at Zolder in April. He then won at Donington, but disaster struck again when he went off into the barriers at Zolder. The race was held after the Formula 1 Grand Prix and the track was covered with treacherous balls of rubber off the racing line. He got one wheel off line and the car spun

● **19**_The start of the European Championship was harder than expected, as was the case here at Hockenheim. Senna became even stronger through learning about defeat, before taking the series by storm.

away and he could not catch it. He was furious with himself for making a mistake, but another element could just as well explain this case of brain fade. The day before the race, Formula 1's most charismatic driver, Gilles Villeneuve, had been killed and there is no doubt that the intense emotion his death provoked had an effect on the young man's concentration. All in all, he European campaign looked like being a difficult one and, when he was caught up in the first lap pile-up in the next round at Hockenheim, the situation looked critical. He had just been caught up in the points by his rival Calvin Fish, who saw here some possible consolation for his impotence in the national series. Adding fuel to the fire of hope was the fact that the Brazilian had shown on two separate occasions that he too was capable of making mistakes. Sadly for the rest of them, they were his last.

He went on to crucify the opposition in the last five races in typical Ayrton style: that is to say, start from pole, take the lead, build up an impossible advantage, all ending on the top step of the podium for this man who surprised and amazed everyone who watched him. At Zandvoort, for the fifth leg, he once again demonstrated his amazing capacity to improvise and adapt to any situation. After a minor mechanical problem, he was unable to take part in the first practice session at the Dutch circuit, where he had never raced before. In the second session, he hung onto the coat tails of a more experienced driver to learn the lines. It then took him six laps to secure pole position!

Of course, it was not long before there were plenty of brave souls queuing up to offer their services to the new little pearl. The first to step forward was Ireland's Eddie Jordan, then running a handy F3 outfit which bore his name, now the boss of a high profile Formula 1 team. He persuaded Ayrton to try a Formula 3 car on Silverstone's Club Circuit. Senna did thirty eight laps and got to within a hundredth of a second of the best time set in the last race held there a few weeks earlier. Jordan was not the sort to miss an opportunity and realised immediately what he was dealing with. He immediately pulled out a contract for the 1983 season, but the Brazilian turned him down. The Irish team was relatively new and Ayrton preferred to concentrate on the rest of his two championships to wait and see what other offers might come along from better established outfits. Then, Dick Bennetts, boss of West Surrey Racing offered him a run in a Ralt-Toyota F3 with a view to racing it at Thruxton on 13th November in a non-championship event. He weighed up the options. He knew the Bennetts test was a great opportunity given that the team's driver, none other than Enrique Mansilla had won five times that year. Senna had raced against Mansilla the previous year in FF 1600 and did not rate his ability at setting up a car, so he reckoned the team must be pretty good if it managed to get him first past the flag. Bennetts admits being knocked out by the young man's lap times, especially as they were done on used tyres. The race was filmed by the BBC and most opportunely, Ayrton pulled out his party piece, taking pole position, winning the race and setting a new lap record along the way. It was therefore perfectly natural that he raced in Formula 3 in 1983 for Dick Bennetts' West Surrey Racing. Perfectly natural, or maybe not, given that Ayrton had said no to one of the top Formula 1 team owners.

BANDEN bv
IJMUIDEN
Tel 02550-11730

Coca-Cola

CHICO SERRA

BRASILINV

PIRELLI

Valvoline

• **20**_The 1982 European events gave Ayrton the chance to experience the world of Formula 1. At Zandvoort, he is seen with the "family" on the start grid, along with his mentor Emerson Fittipaldi, boss of the team which bore his name and his friend Chico Serra. Unfortunately for the Brazilian clan, Chico retired and "Emmo's" team shut up shop at the end of the season.

Having set McLaren on the road to success since taking over the reins in 1980, the ambitious Ron Dennis offered to finance the young Senna da Silva's F3 season, in exchange for an option on a McLaren contract which would give him exclusive rights to the young prodigy's services. But the young prodigy was having none of it. He didn't want an option, he wanted a guaranteed drive and Dennis was not prepared to guarantee that. Ayrton dug his heels in and the experienced team boss had to admit he was beaten. He had underestimated the driver's strength of character and he would recall these discussions when the two men met a few years later to discuss their common future once again. For his part, Ayrton stayed true to his principles and was not about to rush his career. He had given Ron Dennis the same answer he had given Murray Taylor a year earlier when he was offered the chance to go straight from FF 1600 to F3.

Back in Brazil for a rejuvenating holiday at the end of the year, he still found time to take part in his last kart race at Porto Alegre to wipe out the disappointment of Kalmar, as covered in chapter 3. He then got down to business with the help of Armando Botelho Teixeira to compile the financial dossier for the coming season, as it required some heavier investment than the small sponsors who had so far come on board. Already present in 1982, the Banerj de São Paulo bank increased its support, joined by a brand of jeans called Pool. Ayrton was thus able to confirm to Dick Bennetts that he would indeed drive for him in 1983, before going off water skiing, sea fishing and resting, to build up his strength for a fight that looked like being even tougher than anything he had experienced to date. ∎

● **21**_A great premier! Ayrton tests Eddie Jordan's F3 car at Silverstone in June 1982. The Irish manager (with woolly hat) did all he could to convince the young prodigy to drive for him in 1983. But Senna felt it was too early in the season to make a decision.

Chapter 6
The doorway to glory

• 22_On the Silverstone podium, 30th May: Senna is jubilant and Martin Brundle manages a smile. The Brazilian had just taken his ninth consecutive win of the season! Later, competition with the Englishman driving for Jordan would become much less amicable.

1983 was a crucial year for Ayrton. Formula 3 is regarded as the first category where a driver really gets to grips with a racing car worthy of the name. Compared with a Formula Ford machine where, in simple terms, all a driver has to do is sit in the cockpit and drive as well as possible, an F3 car has a number of parameters which can be adjusted to alter the handling. The tyres are softer and offer more grip and their performance can be altered by subtle tuning of the inflation pressures. The wings are adjustable to alter the amount of downforce on the car, the ride heights can be played with and the suspension also offers more adjustment. Ayrton demonstrated his total mastery of this new challenge when he won at Thruxton the previous November, but now he put himself under even more pressure to move up a notch in terms of his understanding of this black art. He enjoyed a perfect understanding with Dick Bennetts, both men being on the same wavelength. The technical briefings were long and instructive, with information flowing in both directions to a far greater extent than had been the case the previous year, when the English team boss had worked with Mansilla.

At the first round of the Marlboro British Formula 3 Championship at Silverstone, Ayrton demonstrated a trait that would mark his career and contribute to the legend that surrounds him, namely the fact he hated not being fastest. He was head and shoulders above the rest in practice, but in qualifying it was an unknown outsider who helped himself to pole position. Senna was only second and spitting bullets. He was convinced that the team which had taken the top slot had done so by cheating and he made his feelings known. He was determined to show everyone who was best and applied plenty of aggression to take the lead on the opening lap, after which he kept it to the chequered flag, which he took with an enormous lead. He had set the tone.

His extreme driving style made its mark over the next few rounds and everyone was worried the championship was turning into a dull procession. On the eve of the ninth of twenty races, he had taken all the wins and every pole position bar the first one. On top of that, he had pulverised the record for most wins (8) set in 1978 by Nelson Piquet. His closest rival was the Englishman Martin Brundle, who drove for the Eddie Jordan team, who despite everything had

just about managed to hang on and was not too far behind. However, the second half of the series produced a scenario full of excitement and sensation, which no one had dared hope for at this point in the season.

The ferocity of the fight between Senna and Brundle increased in inverse proportion to the distance between the two cars on the track. Ayrton began to commit sins of pride and Martin managed to snaffle pole position from him and the affair turned nasty when the Englishman punted the Brazilian off the track at Snetterton in July. From then on, Senna's thoughts centred on

revenge for what he considered an assassination attempt. In terms of serenity, he did not have much left in the bank. Dick Bennetts was also worried, as the championship which had started off so well was now turning in favour of the Jordan team, who were certainly not interested in pouring oil on troubled waters. No doubt this had something to do with the fact Eddie had been turned down by Senna when he offered him a drive.

Despite two dominant wins at Silverstone, in July and August, Ayrton's performance had dropped over the summer, basically because of

CADERNETA DE POUPANÇA
BANERJ

• **24**_After an uncertain second half of the season, Ayrton Senna brought his time in Formula 3 to a close in the best way possible on 23rd October at Thruxton, winning the race and taking the title.

this obsession with "justice" which haunted his soul. He finally assuaged his thirst for vengeance at Oulton Park in September, but he was hoisted by his own petard as he set a trap for his opponent which ended with one car on top of the other, after they collided at high speed! Fortunately, both drivers emerged unscathed, but finally the stewards decided to put an end to this dangerous duel. They hit Senna with a fine and a warning on his license, while Brundle got away with a verbal warning, but no fine. It was not what Ayrton wanted to comfort his sense of injustice, which he felt so deeply.

But for this prickly reaction to what he regarded as an affront to his authority, he would have picked up a few easy wins, or at least some important points for the championship. But that was Ayrton: a man who refused to admit he was not always the best. It would take him many years to deal with these demons and only much later, towards the end of his career, did he calm down a bit. For those who knew him well, the demons were ever present, but by then, his race craft had improved and that prompted him to ease off when he had to. It is hard to analyse the conscious or unconscious reasons which pushed him to these excesses. To a certain extent it was down to the targets he set himself, which meant that nothing less than victory was ever good enough for him, and which he felt was his due because of all the hard work he had invested. Pride also came into the equation, but all great champions need that in order to believe in themselves and give that little bit extra. However, his desire for perfection knew no bounds and he could not put up with anything that got between him and excellence. A perfect lap spoilt by a "nobody" who had not seen the blue flags would really get him fired up. It is significant to note

that this new aggressive attitude only came to the fore this year, when the car did not react the way he had expected. In 1981 and '82 he had encountered virtually no real opposition. But that was no longer the case in 1983.

It all came down to a final shoot-out on 23rd October at the last race at Thruxton. Having retired at the same track the previous month with a broken engine and only finishing second behind Brundle at Silverstone, he was tackling the final round as the challenger! He had indeed lost the series lead, but luckily his motivation got a major boost, which was sorely needed. He got a grip of himself mentally and found a reserve of strength to nail down his opponent. The public saw the great Senna once again, apparently lost in his own personal maelstrom, but on his way to an incontestable triumph. Martin Brundle admits that on that day the Brazilian was once again untouchable. In the end, Ayrton Senna won the British Formula 3 championship and then went on to take a superb international win in the streets of Macau at the end of the season. It brought a rare trilogy to a close with a masterly flourish. It was fitting reward for an exceptional driver who could see the doors to his dreams opening before him.

Ever since he returned to England at the start of the previous season, Ayrton Senna thought of little else but Formula 1. He had promised himself not to accept any offers to get there in less than ideal conditions. But now he felt ready for it. It is a tradition for Formula 1 team owners to test a few likely candidates in the course of the season, to check out the new wave which might swell the ranks of the existing drivers. Thanks to extensive media coverage of his exploits, Ayrton naturally received his fair share of offers to have a trial run. Frank Williams called him up to try the FW08 in July at Donington. Senna willingly accepted the invitation and he adapted so quickly to this powerful machine that, during a break, Frank made sure the fuel cell was filled up to slow him down a bit, so that other team owners present that day would not realise just how quick was this new Brazilian. Williams was definitely impressed with his turn of speed on the day, but decided to wait a while before making a decision. It was an error of judgement which would take him eleven years to put right. At the end of the season, Ayrton went off to do his shopping. He had several requests from F1 team bosses keen to find a young and promising driver for 1984. He therefore took part in three tests: McLaren and Toleman at Silverstone and Brabham at Paul Ricard. With Niki Lauda and Alain Prost on the books, Ron Dennis knew he had a more than complete driver line-up, but he was still keen to get a close look at the young man who had stood toe to toe with him the previous year. Later he remembered being struck by the determination of the young man at one point during the test. Just as he was getting down to some serious lap times, the Cosworth engine began to tighten up. Dennis wanted to stop the test there, but Senna begged him to set up another one has he had not had time to do a quick lap.

A few days later, Ayrton was back at the Northamptonshire circuit to get behind the wheel of the Hart turbo-powered Toleman 183. This was a new experience for Senna, as he discovered the kick in the pants power of a turbocharger. The technology introduced by Renault in 1977 was now used by all the major players, but the four

cylinder Hart engine in the Toleman was not very sophisticated and the power delivery was brutal. The car was heavy and not very competitive, but by the end of the day, Senna was lapping quicker than Derek Warwick and Bruno Giacomelli, the 1983 drivers, who would not be invited back for the following season. Team boss Alex Hawkridge was pleased to see that his judgement had been correct. Of course, he had followed the Brazilian's progress with interest since his FF1600 days and he was delighted with what he saw that November day on the Silverstone grand prix circuit. If he acted quickly, he could get his hands on F1's new prodigy. Ted and Bob Toleman owned the biggest car transport business in England and in 1970 set up a race team with Hawkridge. Having gradually moved up the racing ladder, one step at a time, including winning the European F2 championship in 1980, they came into Formula 1 in 1981, along with their engine supplier from the previous year, Brian Hart and his brand new four cylinder turbocharged engine. After struggling initially, Toleman's team was finally taking off and was now regarded as a team of the future, with a solid base and plenty of potential. It was just the thing to attract a young driver who wanted to grow alongside a team. The fledgling nature of the operation meant there would be less pressure than in a top team. On the very next day after the test, Alex Hawkridge got his lawyers to draw up a contract which he wanted to get Senna to sign as quickly as possible. The Brabham test only served to broaden the Brazilian's experience of a Formula 1 car, as there seemed to be little chance for 1984 that Ayrton could join the team run by Formula 1's

● **25**_On 27ᵗʰ November, Ayrton won in the narrow twisty streets of Macau in this Marlboro Ralt, entered by Chinese millionaire Teddy Yip. It was his final glory title before taking the big leap into Formula 1.

● **26-27 and 28**_The most important exam of his career. At the end of the season, Ayrton tried various Formula 1 cars (from top to bottom:) the Williams FW08 with Frank Williams in white shirt; the Brabham BT52 with Bernie Ecclestone in jacket and Gordon Murray making notes and finally, the McLaren MP4-1 with Ron Dennis explaining the programme, while Martin Brundle (standing, in Marlboro jacket) also present for a test, makes sure he does not miss a trick. In the end, Ayrton went for the least famous option, signing for Toleman in 1984.

Mr. Big, Bernie Ecclestone. Officially, the team's Italian sponsor, Parmalat, wanted an Italian driver to partner 1983 world champion, Brazil's Nelson Piquet. Unofficially, Nelson had made it clear to Bernie that he would be off like a shot if he had to cohabit with the Paulista.

Piquet's aversion to Senna is no secret. Nelson is a "Carioca," the name given to residents of Rio and there is a bitter rivalry between inhabitants of Brazil's two biggest cities. On top of that, despite his achievements, the whimsical Nelson could never match the great Emerson's popularity. And now it seemed that Senna was about to follow "Emmo" in the popularity stakes, with Nelson the loser in the affair. He was definitely out of sorts and made a point of blanking Ayrton's exploits to date. When the young man was taken by Fittipaldi to meet him on a courtesy visit to a grand prix in 1982, Nelson ignored him as only he could. In one sense it did him no favours, as Senna swore with all the strength of character one can imagine, that he would take great pleasure in beating the man on the track. Naturally that day did come and the hatred between the two of them never faltered. The situation got tawdry in 1988, when a particularly poorly inspired Piquet suggested during an interview with a Brazilian newspaper that Senna was homosexual, stating that "one never sees him with a woman." Now is not the time to go into personal details, but suffice it to say that Ayrton had various liaisons with beautiful girlfriends, some of them quite serious later in his life. However, unlike Nelson he did not make a point of showing them off in public. Piquet was far more of a dilettante and his motivation behind the wheel of a racing car could be questionable. His personal credibility took a major knock as Ayrton's star rose to the Olympian heights of a great champion. Piquet was the only Brazilian driver who did not attend Ayrton's funeral in 1994 and at least in this respect, he stayed true to himself and the public to the very end.

Back to the subject in hand, Ayrton Senna had made his choice. On 19th December 1983, he signed a ten page contract, tying him to the Toleman team for three years. At that moment in time, this long term deal held no fears for the youngster. On the contrary, it meant he would have plenty of time to learn and evolve along with his team. The salary was not exactly huge, but the contract allowed for that to be changed if he started getting good results. For the moment, Senna was delighted with what he had. As this year came to an end, only one thing mattered to him and that was the coming season. He would be driving a Formula 1 car alongside some of the best drivers in the world. ■

The eyewitness account of Lionel Froissart

As someone who knew him well, Lionel Froissart was aware that Ayrton was not prepared to start a family while he was risking his life on the race track.

"He made the mistake of getting married very young. The way he operated, he could not deal with the fact he was a married man. Liliane and he had been friends for a long time and she used to come to the kart tracks. But it didn't work at all because, on the one hand, he was bringing a Brazilian girl to the back of beyond in England, where the weather was foul and on top of that he had his job to do. She spent whole days just waiting at the track. Frankly, it was not what she had dreamed of. So it was obvious really.
But he did realise very quickly that starting a family was a serious business and he was not prepared to do both at the same time. Racing took up 120% of his thoughts and that sense of balance that some people get from marriage, Ayrton already had it through his family. It was all he needed and he could not get more involved. But he did love children and was besotted with his little nephews. But as for kids of his own, he wanted to wait until his career was over, as he was aware of the risks and in one sense, he did the right thing. He had a dangerous job and, despite what a lot of people think, he was well aware of the dangers. He was not stupid, quite the contrary and he did not want to risk putting a family through the loss of a father and a husband."

• **29**_Ayrton in 1993 with his girlfriend Adriana Galisteu.

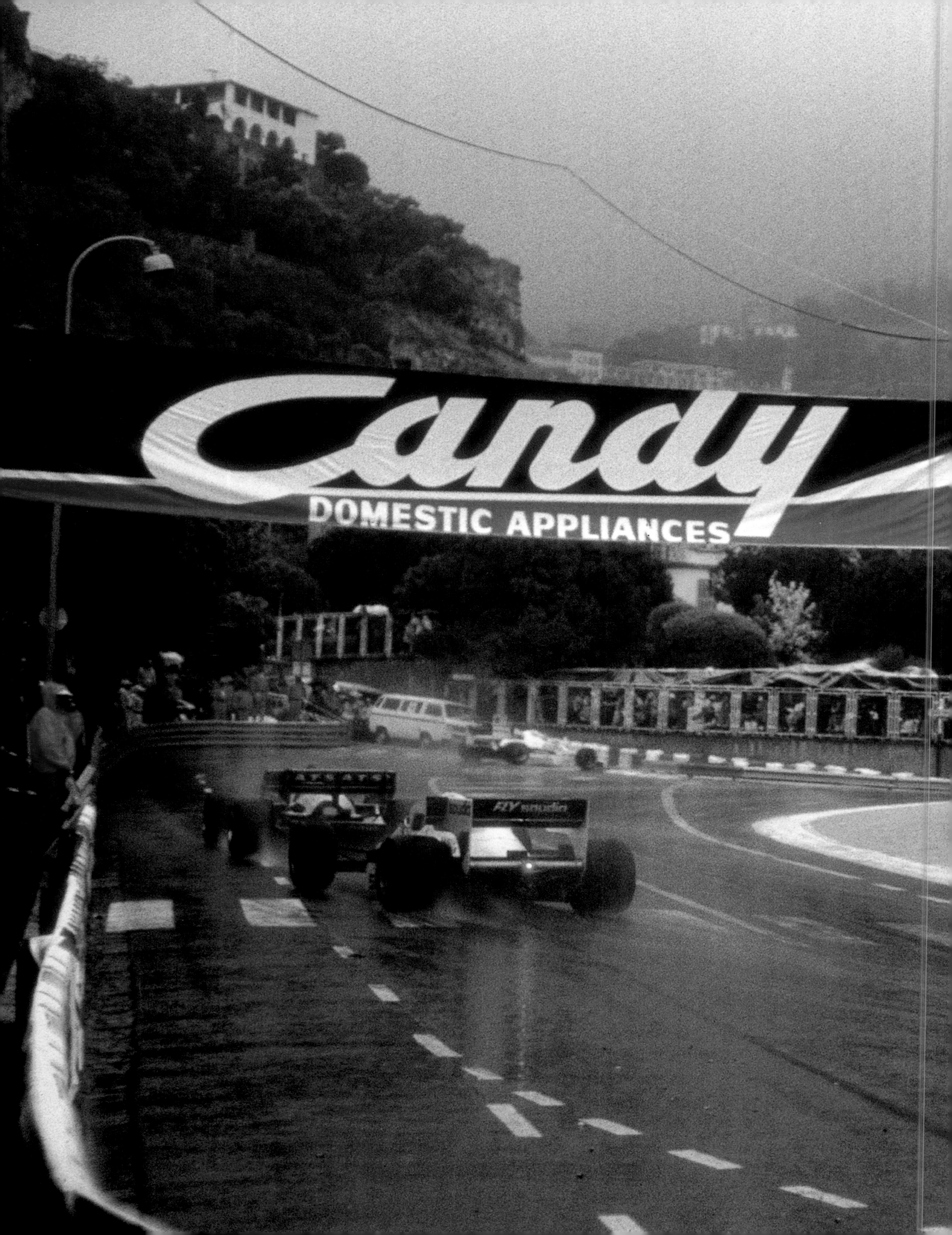
Candy
DOMESTIC APPLIANCES

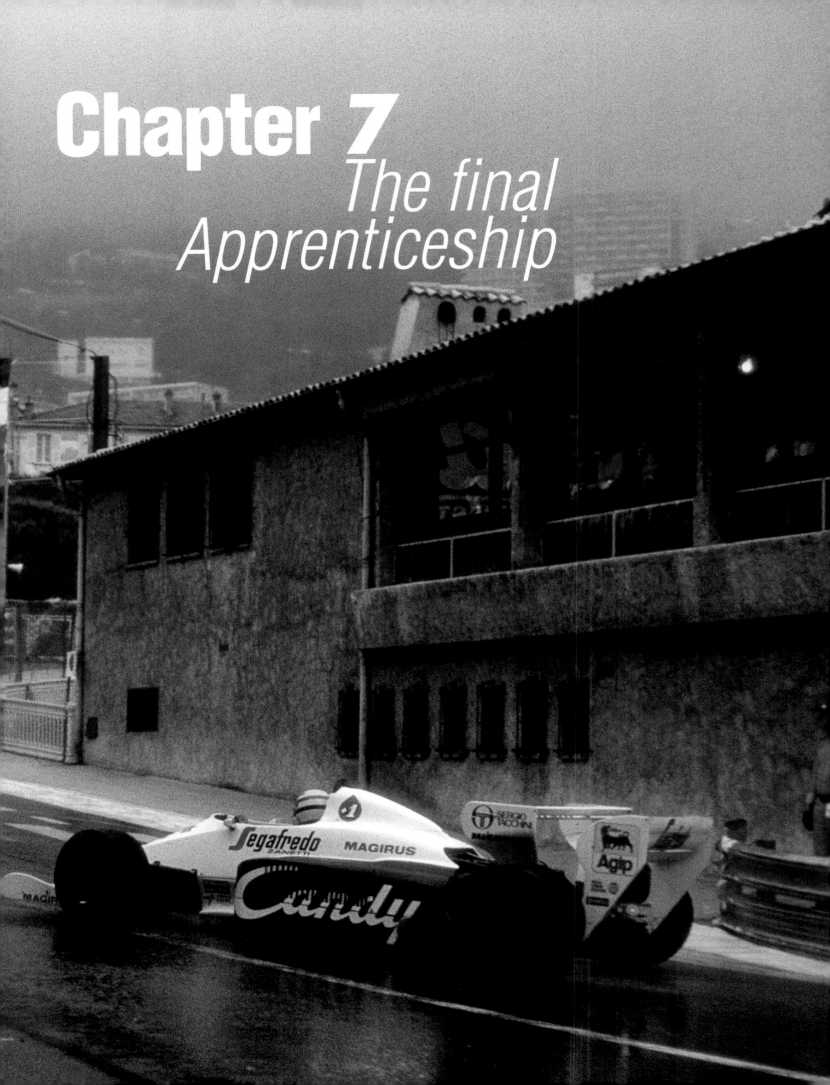

Chapter 7
The final Apprenticeship

• **30**_The Brazilian made his mark in Formula 1, scoring a point at Kyalami in an unstable car minus part of its bodywork. Behind Senna is his team-mate Johnny Cecotto.

Ayrton Senna was well aware that he had just made it into the best and the worst of worlds. The best because Formula 1 represents the pinnacle of a professional driver's career, the highest and most demanding point in terms of performance and experience; the worst because, as of now, he was at the bottom of the ladder and would no longer win almost every Sunday, as he had been in the habit of doing up to a few months previously. If he or his team stagnated, that would be it until the following year.

Ayrton had no doubts as to his own ability and anything less than total confidence would have been unexpected. He also had faith in his team, but the difference in terms of weaponry did surprise him during the first FOCA test at Rio in January 1984. All the teams had turned out at the Jacarepagua circuit to prepare for the forthcoming season which was due to kick off at this very track in a couple of months. The facts of life were rammed home with a bang for the young driver. In no other form of motorsport is there such a gap between the haves and the

have-nots. Toleman was obviously in the second category, but everyone in the team, including Ayrton, was prepared to do whatever it took to make it to the premiere division as quickly as possible. But even among the poorer teams, some were worse off than others and that is what disappointed the Brazilian. He immediately realised that his car was a bit of a dog. The basic design of the TG183B had been penned by Rory Byrne at the end of 1982 with all the negatives that entailed. Its Pirelli tyres proved very inconsistent and lacked pace. The turbocharged four cylinder engine designed by Brian Hart, who was an excellent engineer, was still put together on a shoestring budget and was far from being fully developed. The power came in with a bang after a long period of turbo lag. Along with a general lack of grip, it was not exactly an encouraging prospect. His team mate that year was Johnny Cecotto, a motorcycle champion who had come to try his luck, following in the footsteps of John Surtees in the Sixties and Mike Hailwood ten years later. On 25th March, the Brazilian Grand Prix confirmed everything Senna

P. MENARD

Designers: Rory Byrne and John Gentry

Engine

Make/Type: Hart 415T
Number of Cylinders/Configuration: in line 4 (Rear)
Capacity: 1496 cc
Bore/Stroke: 88 x 61.5 mm
Compression ratio: 6.7 : 1
Turbo(s): 1, Holset
Maximum power: 600 hp
Maximum revs: 10750 rpm
Block material: Aluminium
Injection: Hart/BRA
Valve gear: 2 OHC
Number of valves per cylinder: 4
Ignition: Marelli
Fuel/Oil: AGIP
Sparking plugs: Champion
Weight (without intercoolers): 131.5 kg

Transmission

Gearbox/Number of gears: Toleman/Hewland (5)
Clutch: Borg&Beck

Chassis

Type: Carbon monocoque
Suspension: Wishbones, pullrods, dampers (Front and Rear)
Shock absorbers: Koni
Rim diameter: 13" (Front and Rear)
Rim width: 11.5" (Front) / 17" (Rear)
Tyres: Pirelli
Brakes: Lockheed discs

Dimensions

Wheelbase: 2692 mm
Track: 1835 mm (Front) / 1683 mm (Rear)
Dry weight: 540 kg
Fuel capacity: 220 litres

Raced from Brazil to San Marino.

had discovered during January testing, in terms of both the chassis and the engine. The tyres were a disaster, with a faulty batch which could not be changed once it had been marked up. In qualifying, Ayrton had to cope with seeing half the grid start ahead of him, whereas in the past he always led the pack. However, he was able to establish one important piece of data: his team-mate was behind him and almost two seconds slower! In motor racing, your first opponent is your team-mate, who has the same equipment to offer a good basis for comparison. Between the two South Americans, the pecking order had been set! Senna's race was cut short by a broken turbo rotor, which dropped the compression and the spirits of part of the crowd which had come to cheer on the Paulista. In South Africa, he finished sixth and picked up an important point. Not everyone manages to finish in the points in his second grand prix, but to do it in a

notoriously heavy car, missing a piece of bodywork after a collision with a piece of debris was quite a feat and one that did not go unnoticed by many, including team bosses. Ayrton noted that he had climbed from the cockpit in a pretty poor state. Driving the unbalanced car had certainly taken its toll, but the frail Brazilian realised there was something he had forgotten to take into account: driving a Formula 1 car for a grand prix distance was much tougher than anything he had encountered in the lower formulae. A driver needs to be strong and have plenty of endurance. When it was pointed out to him, Senna who did not like being told what to do in any area of his life, rejected the accusation and claimed he was in fine form. But from then on, he put himself through a daily fitness programme which built up his muscle bulk and his endurance.

Back from South Africa, the Toleman team headed for Brands Hatch to test the new 184T. Senna found it much more accommodating than its predecessor, but the team turned up at Zolder on 29th April with two 183T. The official reason was only revealed a week later at the San Marino Grand Prix. While all the other teams were engaged in the first free practice session at the Imola circuit, the Toleman drivers were the victims of a technical strike! Ted Toleman had forbidden the team to touch their toolkits until the Pirelli situation was sorted. The Toleman-Pirelli marriage was heading for the rocks of divorce, as the English team blamed its Italian supplier for its poor performance to date and was openly looking towards Michelin, which supplied amongst others, top teams like McLaren and Brabham. In fact, a secret contract had already been signed between the two parties and the 184T had been designed around the Clermont-Ferrand rubber. But admitting to it too early would have prejudiced the deal, which explained the delay in bringing out the 184T.

Ayrton was definitely happy with the planned change, but was equally upset at having to twiddle his thumbs when he would have liked to be out on the circuit learning a track he had never visited before. An agreement was finally reached late in the evening and the drivers finally took to the track on Saturday. Cecotto just managed to squeeze onto the back of the grid, but Senna was forced to watch the race on television in the press room with the Brazilian journalists. The injection system on his engine had malfunctioned throughout the second qualifying session and he was unable to set a time.

There was no doubt that the switch to Michelin boosted morale within the team. Of course, Toleman did not get the pick of the tyres, which went to McLaren and Brabham, but the general opinion was that even the previous year's Michelins were better than any Pirellis. The 184T also got a warm reception. The 183T had been a nightmare for the team. But welcome as it was, the new car did not provide an instant fix to the team's problems. However, the Toleman did

● **31**_Senna briefs the Toleman designer, the South African Rory Byren (on right) who would later work with Michael Schumacher at Benetton and Ferrari.

● **32**_The Toleman is refuelled in the pits at Detroit, watched by Brian Hart, who hopes his 4 cylinder turbo engine will bring a victory for the team and its favourite driver.

P. MÉNARD

Designers: Rory Byrne and John Gentry

Engine

Make/Type: Hart 415T
Number of Cylinders/Configuration: in line 4 (Rear)
Capacity: 1496 cc
Bore/Stroke: 88 x 61.5 mm
Compression ratio: 6.7 : 1
Turbo(s): 1, Holset
Maximum power: 600 hp
Maximum revs: 10750 rpm
Block material: Aluminium
Fuel/Oil: AGIP
Sparking plugs: Champion
Injection: Hart/BRA
Valve gear: 2 OHC
Number of valves per cylinder: 4
Ignition: Marelli
Weight (without intercoolers): 131.5 kg

Transmission

Gearbox/Number of gears: Toleman/Hewland (5)
Clutch: Borg&Beck

Chassis

Type: Carbon monocoque
Suspension: Wishbones, pullrods, dampers (Front), Double wishbones, pushrods, springs (Rear)
Shock absorbers: Koni
Rim diameter: 13" (Front and Rear)
Rim width: 11.8" (Front) / 16.25" (Rear)
Tyres: Michelin
Brakes: Brembo

Dimensions

Wheelbase: 2692 mm
Track: 1816 mm (Front) / 1683 mm (Rear)
Dry weight: 540 kg
Fuel capacity: 220 litres

Raced from France to Portugal.

improve and its Brazilian driver did not miss the chance to shine whenever an opportunity presented itself. The first of these came at Monaco and it was the race which put Ayrton on the map.

The Principality was a step into the unknown for the Brazilian as he had not raced here in Formula 3 because of tyre problems. The legendary street circuit with its twists and turns is like no other track on earth. Although average speeds are slow it will not forgive the slightest error, with the ever present barriers waiting to trap the unwary. In the first free practice session, Ayrton did his first ten laps at a pace which would have been embarrassing in a Formula Ford, before flooring the throttle in fully confident mode. He set out to learn everything; the bumps, the manhole covers, the blinding light on the exit to the tunnel at more than 250 km/h. Come race day there was no chance of being dazzled by the sun as large cumulonimbus clouds hung above the harbour

and the rain lashed down. Ayrton started from the middle of the grid in a huge cloud of spray with virtually no visibility on a very slippery track. Cecotto spun off on the opening lap while Senna analysed the situation and was wary of everything, operating the throttle with the lightest of touches. To reduce the danger of a sudden boost of power, he turned the turbo down to its minimum setting, knocking off the power. The car was now easier to driver and, bit by bit, the Toleman no. 19 began passing other cars at the rate of about one per lap. There was no sign of the rain easing off and in fact it got heavier. Third on lap 16, Ayrton moved up to second on lap 19 when Niki Lauda retired the McLaren. Ahead of him by a few seconds was Alain Prost in the other McLaren. The spectators were mesmerised, suddenly realising that the insignificant blue and white Toleman was catching the leader like a rocket.

Prost was obviously in difficulty, his brakes were locking up and he knew the race was lost if it went the distance. Meanwhile, race director Jacky Ickx, who knew a thing or two about rain decided that conditions were now ridiculous and that to continue was folly, as over half the cars had retired and the race had not even reached half distance. At the very moment when he decided to wave the chequered flag to signal the end of the race, he saw Senna splash by, having just passed Prost a few metres earlier. The young Paulista was convinced he had won!

The rules state that if a race is stopped before full distance, then the final order is taken from the penultimate lap. At that point, Senna was behind Prost. Ayrton could not believe what he heard. It was the pain of Estoril 1979 all over again and he simply shook his head, with a wan smile. But as far as he was concerned and he told his team as much, the powers that be could not cope with the idea of an unknown driver winning the most prestigious Grand Prix ahead of the undoubted favourite. Another injustice had just been committed.

The Brazilian Federation was caught up in a Latin fury and complained about Jacky Ickx, who received a warning from the FISA, but no action was taken against him. Ayrton chose to ignore three elements to this tale: first of all, he could

have been on the long list of non-finishers as he had a miraculous escape after flying over a kerb in the early stages. Secondly, he was not the only man flying that day, as just behind him the promising Stefan Bellof was going even quicker in the Tyrrell and was closing fast. Ken Tyrrell was equally furious about the early end to the race. His was the only normally aspirated car on the grid and therefore the easiest to drive in the conditions. Who is to say if the Brazilian would have won if Ickx had not stopped the race. Finally, Ayrton's desire to win at all costs meant he failed to see how his performance had been well received by all the experts. The fans too had just discovered a fantastic driver and team owners could talk of little else.

The North American rounds which followed Monaco were very frustrating for Ayrton who failed to pick up any points and realised just what a gap there was between his team and the star players. At the same time, he was becoming more aware of his own potential and that of his team. Manifestly, Toleman would not be able to give him what he wanted, at least in the short term. And Ayrton was increasingly anxious to snick his career into top gear by winning races. His mind went back to the Friday in Imola when, out of work because of the Pirelli-Toleman crisis, he had been courted by Peter Warr. The Team

● **33**_On 31ˢᵗ May on the Monaco skating rink, the young prodigy really arrived on the Formula 1 scene: he was the rain master.

• **34**_After an over-anxious start at the Nürburgring, Senna has just caused havoc at the first corner.

Eyewitness account of Pierre Dupasquier

Pierre Dupasquier joined Michelin in 1962, to take charge of the F1, GT, Rally and Motorcycle programmes from 1973 to 1984, before taking overall charge of the competitions department in 1996. He is an enthusiastic professional and an expert on all forms of motor sport. He remembers the 1984 Monaco Grand Prix:
"It was the first time we had supplied the Toleman team. Our engineer who looked after them came to see me. "There's a young lad there who came up with some amazing suggestions and now he wants to see you." It was Ayrton. He came to our little caravan and started to go through the track corner by corner. I was amazed, because on a first attempt at this circuit all you concentrate on is not hitting the barriers! But he seemed to have dealt with that already and spent his time in a very subtle and pertinent analysis of each corner. His comments were very interesting and professional. He did not know Monaco, doing his first laps very slowly, before picking up the pace, given that his car had a very good chassis which was penalised by a lack of power from the engine. It meant he had a very clear picture of every part of the track, which was totally amazing for a young lad who was new to it all. He was a bit like a great artist or a conductor, who was sealed into his own little world knocking out Shostakovich or Mahler. When a conductor prepares to perform a symphony, he is totally immersed in it and that was the case with Ayrton. He concentrated intensely on what he was doing, locking himself into the grand prix. All the greats are like that, but with him, you could see it straight away. He could maintain extremely high levels of involvement and concentration."

Eyewitness account of Lionel Froissart

Over the years, Ayrton Senna and Lionel Froissart became close as they got to know one another. Senna knew he could trust the French journalist, which was important for a man so keen to protect his and his family's privacy.

"Like all great champions who know their worth and are not very modest, Senna never doubted he was a great driver. He could appear very sure of himself, as happened after his performance at Monaco in 1984. I can understand that some people take that to be arrogance, but in fact, I very quickly realised that he needed to distance himself from all these people who suddenly wanted to be his friend. When you become a star, you suddenly have lots of mates who like you, who are very friendly towards you. Ayrton suddenly found himself much in demand and this was just a way for him to protect himself. It's understandable, as if you get caught up in all the adulation, it can soon turn against you.
In my opinion, his biggest fault was his sense of paranoia. He'd say, "what do these people want from me? Where do they want to take me." I watched him have rows with journalists who were too pushy. It didn't happen often, but he could lose his cool. He was quite impulsive."

Lotus boss had been keeping an eye on Ayrton since the end of 1983 and would have liked to have him on board for this season. But JPS, the team's principal sponsor wanted a British driver alongside Elio de Angelis and so Nigel Mansell saved his seat for 1984. Certain he would not have to meet this condition for 1985, Peter Warr had therefore gone in pursuit of Senna as early as possible in the season so as not to lose the chance of signing up the man he already described as "the little Mozart of Formula 1." Ayrton was excited by the fact that a top team boss was showing interest, but in his usual way, he did not rush to reach any decision. It was by now the mid-point of the season and the driver transfer market was gaining momentum. Ayrton had already warned Alex Hawkridge that he was dissatisfied and, in private, he expressed doubts as to the ability of his team managers to tackle the huge task they had set themselves. On top of that, the idea of working at Lotus with its technical director Gerard Ducarouge, was a prospect which delighted him. During the FOCA test in Brazil, the Frenchman was taken aback when Ayrton told him he knew everything about his work and was sure that they would collaborate one day. Warr's offer was therefore worth a second look.

Senna finished a superb third in the British Grand Prix on a sunny Sunday 27th July at Brands Hatch. This second podium served to confirm his reputation as a talented newcomer on a track where one needs a well set-up car and a good dose of courage. It proved that his Monegasque performance in the rain was no flash in the pan. In the final stages, the battle he waged and won with the Lotus of Elio de Angelis brought the crowd to its feet and a smile to the face of Peter Warr. The Lotus team boss did not really need this demonstration to convince him that he was right to chase the Brazilian. Events were about to move on apace.

That weekend, in unfortunate circumstances, Ayrton benefited from the undivided attention of his whole team. On the first day of practice, his team-mate Johnny Cecotto had been caught out by the slippery surface and slammed into the barriers at high speed, badly breaking his legs. It meant the end of the former motorcycle champion's Formula 1 career. Senna was inspired around the contours of the Kentish track, but he reacted insensitively to the accident and was the only driver not to visit the Venezuelan in hospital. Relations between the two men had long since been reduced to the bare minimum. According to Cecotto, the Brazilian had been fine with him until he was outpaced at an earlier test session at Donington. From then on, Senna concentrated on being quicker than his team-mate every time they took to the track. He managed that with ease, demoralising Cecotto on the way. But in this

● **35**_Ayrton's expression conveys his frustration at the lack of progress in the Toleman team. He now had to aim higher and he would do that with Lotus.

instance, a bit of humanity would not have gone amiss. It was a conflict which Ayrton would confront several times during his career: how to find the dividing line between total domination on the track and being blind to any form of compassion? Years later, Senna admitted he had been clumsy in the way he handled the situation.

The busy British weekend was followed by three consecutive retirements, as Ayrton's career was about to turn a corner. Like illicit lovers, Senna and Warr met more and more frequently, helped in their tryst by Domingo Piedade, a Portuguese friend of Armando Bothelo Teixeira. The agreement was signed in total secrecy in mid-August, but it was not made public until after the Dutch Grand Prix on the 26th. Despite all these precautions, the rumour was doing the

rounds of the Zandvoort paddock over the weekend and the atmosphere in the Toleman camp was stretched to breaking point. Alex Hawkridge was well aware that his little wonder would not be happy with what he had for much longer and realised it was going to be difficult to hang onto him. But when the news of the move to Lotus for 1985 finally broke cover, he went ballistic. As far as he was concerned, Senna's contract not only tied him to the team for three years, but on top of that, the Brazilian was supposed to pay for an early release to go to another team. The Brazilian denied it all to anyone who was prepared to listen. Ted Toleman felt that these two mistakes would have to be paid for in the only way that would hurt the driver. He quite simply banned him from taking part in the forthcoming Italian Grand Prix at Monza. His car was entrusted to Stefan Johansson for this round. The punishment was simple but effective. Ayrton was devastated and the whole sorry mess tarnished his image. The next race at the new Nürburgring did little to improve matters for the Paulista. Was he still reeling from the shock of the race ban or was he trying just a bit too hard to prove his talent? Whatever, he caused a huge shunt at the start which wrote off five cars, including the Williams of Keke Rosberg, who made his feelings felt in no uncertain terms. As the 1984 season came to a close, Ayrton Senna was regarded as a driver of limitless talent, but his image was tarnished and controversial. The fans loved his antics on the track and were happy to forgive him his off-track excesses. It was a feeling that followed Senna throughout his career.

Another example of his huge talent came at the last round of the season at Estoril. It was the final title showdown between Alain Prost and Niki Lauda and it was also the last grand prix for Michelin, as the French company had decided to pull out of the sport having won all there was to win. "Bibendum's" sporting director, Pierre Dupasquier therefore opened the doors to the tyre trucks, giving away qualifying tyres to all his customers. It was the first time Senna had been allowed to use the "miracle" tyres. The result was instantaneous with Ayrton qualifying third, two tenths off the front row runners, Piquet and Prost. He finished the race third behind the two McLaren stars. The Lotus boys were already looking forward to working with "Mozart," while the Toleman crew could take some consolation from the fact that it was they who had brought him into the sport. In the end, Ayrton Senna and Toleman parted company on good terms, having got over their spat, with both parties aware that the split was inevitable.

For the first time in his career, Ayrton had completed a season without taking a single win. But he knew he had pulled off a victory of sorts. In the ever so elitist world of Formula 1, he had made his mark and signed to drive for one of the most famous team. There was a further more symbolic aspect to this turn of events, in that, twelve years after his idol Fittipaldi, he was about to sit in the cockpit of a black and gold John Player Special, which Emerson had used to take the first of his two world titles. Ayrton had a duty to prove he was worthy of that honour. ■

Eyewitness account of Henri Pescarolo

Like all his contemporaries, Ayrton Senna did not stray far from the world of Formula 1. Except on two occasions, in 1984: he won a celebrity race at the wheel of a road-going Mercedes at the new Nürburgring. Then he joined Henri Pescarolo and Stefan Johansson, still on the same circuit, driving a Joest Porsche in the Endurance Championship (photo.) The trio finished eighth and the great Henri, a four times Le Mans winner was able to appreciate the qualities of the young and introverted driver. *"It was Domingo Piedade, the Portuguese friend of all the Brazilian drivers, who knew Reinhold Joest, who got him the drive. He said to Joest: "You need to see this guy, he's a real rocket." Ayrton was happy to try a new form of racing, driving a big car on a circuit he didn't know. It was good experience for a youngster and a chance to make a name for himself. At the time, people were getting killed. Four or five drivers would pass on and they had to be replaced. For us, it was a natural phenomenon to see young drivers turning up. They replaced those who had gone. It was a normal cycle.*
He arrived seeming very timid, keeping himself to himself, hardly saying a word. But as soon as he got in the car, we understood. He instantly started doing quick lap times. But we didn't know him and had never heard of him. We knew he was Brazilian. I was from the Fittipaldi generation, so anything later than that was a mystery. When we saw him drive, we simply thought, "here's another Brazilian who's going to get talked about soon." On the technical side, he did not have to work on the car. In endurance racing, it is the most experienced driver or the factory driver who decides on the settings. The co-driver just gets in and drives, that's all."

Chapter 8
Hopes of black and gold

● **36**_A truly classic moment:
the first of Ayrton Senna's
41 Formula 1 wins came in the
rain. It happened on 21ˢᵗ April
1985 at Estoril, just yards
away from the venue of his
cruel disappointment in
karting, six years earlier!

It can be argued that there are two Formula 1 teams which lay claim to legendary status: Ferrari and Lotus. The Italian Scuderia for the variety and class of its products as well as its triumphs and the English team for its inventiveness and the new technologies it brought to Grand Prix racing. Both were created by exceptional men. In 1985, the 87 year old Enzo Ferrari was still at the helm in Maranello, but sadly, Colin Chapman died from a heart attack in December 1982. His faithful lieutenant Peter Warr picked up the reins and the following year, appointed Gerard Ducarouge as Technical Director. The Frenchman had been responsible for Matra's successes at Le Mans in the 70s and designed the first Ligier cars (the ones that won.) He was known for his punctilious approach to his work which was just what Lotus needed having gone through several cruelly barren seasons. It last won the world championship in 1978 with Mario Andretti driving the legendary 79 in the days of the ground effect phenomenon, introduced by Chapman and the all-conquering Cosworth V8. Since then, Lotus had won just once, with Elio de Angelis in Austria in 1982. With Ducarouge at the controls and Senna and de Angelis at the wheel, Warr was sure Lotus was about to take off again. Powered by the Renault

V6 turbo, the 95T had shown plenty of potential and the technical director had further refined the car, which became the 97T in 1985.

Of course, Ayrton was aware of the project before signing the contract but ever pragmatic and dubious, he asked to come and visit Ducarouge at Ketteringham Hall, the Lotus HQ. The Brazilian wanted to be sure the Frenchman was on site, knowing that Ron Dennis had been chasing Ducarouge. Once he had seen for himself, he decided to sign on the dotted line.

After a bit of a scare over the winter when he suddenly developed a worrying facial paralysis which luckily was soon treated successfully, Senna came to the Lotus factory for talks with the engineers and mechanics to make some suggestions of his own. Right from the start, he impressed everyone with his incredible determination and the demands he put on himself and others to reach their goals. The Lotus team also had to pay off Toleman for breaking the driver's contract, although the sum involved was actually insignificant. It would not be enough to save the team created by the Toleman brothers. A disastrous financial situation saw it disappear at the end of the season, to be bought out by Benetton.

From the very start of winter testing, Ayrton was reassured to find he had indeed moved up to the higher division and felt he was in with a chance of winning races. The Lotus 97T was in a different league to anything he had driven so far. It was a real top class Formula 1 car. The chassis worked well on its Goodyear tyres and Renault's V6 turbo was a real powerhouse. Towards the end of his career, Ayrton claimed this was the best balanced car he had ever driven. The respect he already had for Ducarouge increased as the two men learnt to work together. The publicity generated by JPS put the team under the spotlight and with the

opening race of the 1985 season taking place in the driver's home country of Brazil, the pressure was intense. Sadly for the Paulista's enthusiastic supporters, his team-mate Elio de Angelis qualified ahead of him and his race ended with an electrical problem. A fortnight later, the next round took place in the land of his Portuguese cousins. Senna had plenty of local support there too and was determined to make up for the disappointment of Rio.

As Spring made a timid appearance, the Estoril circuit was swept by a cold wind which brought the odd spell of drizzle. It was not the warm and bright weather one normally

● **37**_The Team Lotus brains alongside Ayrton's 97T (from left to right:) race engineer, Steve Hallam and his ever present cap, talks with Technical Director Gerard Ducarouge, while team boss Peter Warr (wearing glasses) contemplates the future.

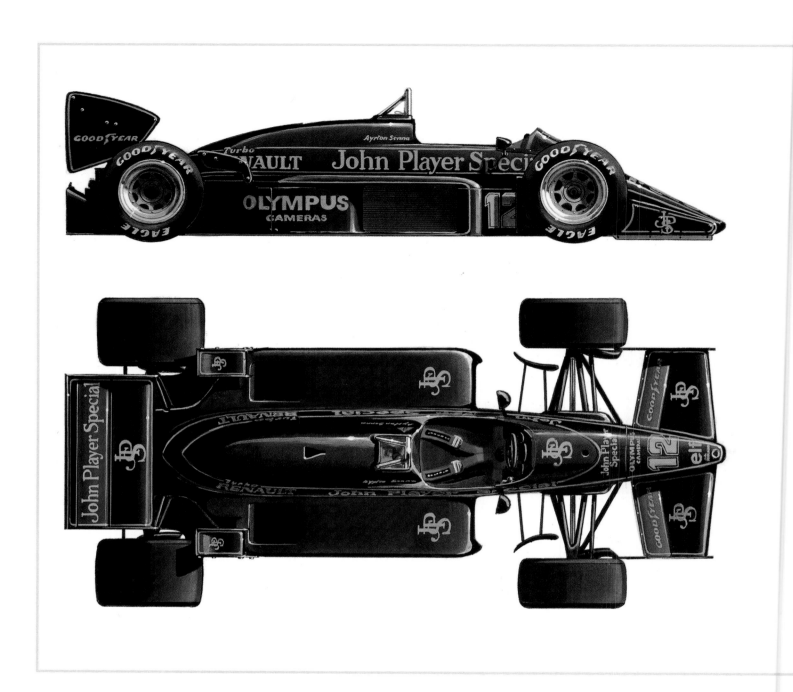

associates with grands prix in this part of the world. To make matters worse, the Lotus' V6 was coughing and grumbling horribly for much of the first practice session and it was only right at the end that the mechanics fixed the problem, caused by a faulty electric pump which provoked a short-circuit in the system. There were only a few minutes remaining and the track was damp. Strapped into the cockpit, Ayrton Senna visualised his qualifying lap before rolling out of pit lane. The V6 roared into life, as its large twin turbos kicked in. The Lotus flowed from kerb to kerb and set the provisional quickest time. The next day, Senna went quicker still and took the first pole position of his short Formula 1 career. What impressed the experts was the way in which he went about his work: maximum

concentration for a minimum amount of time, one lap to have a look-see and then the perfect lap. The Senna Method saw the light of day on this Saturday 20th April and it never changed over the next ten years. Later, Warr admitted he was astounded by the amazing precision of Senna's predictions, telling him the lap time he felt he could do and then go out and get within a tenth of his prediction. Ducarouge was equally impressed and recalls with amusement the tale of the half second advantage gained on paper. One day, Ayrton explained to him where on the lap he could pick up the odd tenth of a second. The engineer ironically replied that if he was true to his word, he would be on pole with a margin of half a second. Senna set off and took pole...with a half second advantage over the rest

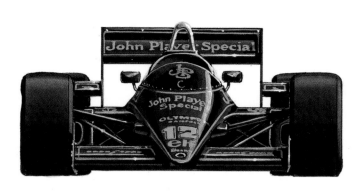

1985 Portugal Grand Prix
Lotus 97T-Renault

P. MÉNARD

Designers: Gérard Ducarouge and Martin Ogilvie

Engine
Make/Type: Renault EF4B/EF15
Number of Cylinders/Configuration: V6 (Rear)
Capacity: 1492 cc (EF4B) / 1494 cc (EF15)
Bore/Stroke: 86 x 42.8 mm (EF4B) /
                    80.1 x 49.4 mm (EF15)
Compression ratio: 7 : 1
Turbo(s): 2, Garrett
Maximum power: 760 hp mm (EF4B) / 810 hp (EF15)
Maximum revs: 11500 rpm
Block material: aluminium
Fuel/Oil: Elf
Sparking plugs: Champion
Injection: Electronic Renix with Weber injectors
Valve gear: 4 OHC
Number of valves per cylinder: 4
Ignition: Marelli
Weight (without intercoolers): 140 kg

Transmission
Gearbox/Number of gears: Lotus/Hewland (5)
Clutch: AP

Chassis
Type: Carbon monocoque
Suspension: Wishbones, pullrods (Front and Rear)
Shock absorbers: Koni
Rim diameter: 13" (Front and Rear)
Rim width: 11.5" (Front) / 16.25" (Rear)
Tyres: Goodyear
Brakes: Brembo/SEP discs

Dimensions
Wheelbase: 2720 mm
Track: 1800 mm (Front) / 1620 mm (Rear)
Dry weight: 540 kg
Fuel capacity: 220 litres

Used all season. Engine: EF4B Brazil and Portugal,
EF15 from San Marino to Australia.

of the pack! Like a member of the audience who returns each night to a cabaret show to try in vain to understand how the magician pulls off his tricks, so too did Ducarouge attempt and fail to understand how his driver did it. But he learnt never to underestimate what the Brazilian said or did. The real magic was reserved for the next day and indeed the word "magic" would soon and forever be linked to the name Ayrton Senna.

On Sunday 21st April, the mist and wind made way for steady rain. The race started under a dusky sky and a soaking wet track. Senna took off prudently in the lead in the Lotus and began to put on a show. While virtually all his rivals, including the big names, went off on the Estoril skating rink, Ayrton put together a series of perfect laps with metronomic regularity. The black and gold JPS seemed to be going round on invisible rails, while the other cars, including his team-mate's seemed to swing from one extreme of oversteer to understeer. Senna won the race as he pleased, finishing over one second ahead of second placed Michele Alboreto in the Ferrari. Just as he did in the lower formulae, he had pulled out one of his "specials," with pole position, the win and fastest race lap. While he did his lap of honour, seat belts off, fists punching the air with delight, his mechanics were led in a dance by Peter Warr, like madmen in front of the grandstands. They were no longer in any doubt that the glory days of the great Lotus team were well and truly back again.

Ayrton realised that his decision to leave Toleman for Lotus had been the right one and his

• **38**_At Spa in 1985, Ayrton gave it his best shot in qualifying, as usual, but was beaten to pole by a tenth of a second by Alain Prost. He made up for it in the race, getting the best start and controlling the foibles of the Renault V6 on the slippery Spa-Francorchamps switchback.

delight as he stepped from the cockpit was a pleasure to see. But it did not take long for his analytical head to regain control over his heart. Speaking to journalists after the race, he admitted he had not driven a perfect race and had almost gone off the track at one point. Once the young lad's joy had settled, the demands of an ambitious and serious young man resurfaced.

From that day on, Senna joined the very exclusive club of future world champions. It was obvious that "the magician" would do it one day, the only question was when. In terms of pure performance, he proved his skill in the next few races, taking pole positions or at least getting near the front of the grid, except in Austria, where engine bothers prevented him from mounting an attack at the right moment. He had shown what he could do and made sure people knew about it. Elio de Angelis was an excellent driver, talented and quick, as well as being a true gentleman. He had secured some good results with Lotus, but his determination and motivation had its ups and downs and was no match for Senna's. At the end of the year, Elio decided to move on to Brabham and sadly was killed in testing in 1986.

Ayrton had to put up with no less than seven consecutive retirements after his Portuguese triumph. No need to point out that any aspirations as to the title had long gone. It was mainly down to the Renault engine which, while being very powerful, was not reliable enough over a race distance. That black run came to an end in Austria, where he finished second, then third in Holland followed by another second in Italy. As long as the parts held together under the vicious 800 odd horsepower from the V6 engine, then Senna was in the hunt. He took his second win of the year at the spectacular Belgian circuit of Spa-Francorchamps, the scene of many great moments in a glorious past. On Saturday, under sunny skies, Alain Prost had cruised to pole position in his McLaren-TAG Porsche, but on the Sunday, the traditional Ardennes rain turned up to shuffle the deck. The Frenchman was not up for taking any risks as the title looked to be his for the taking and Ayrton went past him at the start, before heading off on a solo run which led to the top step of the podium.

It was during this grand prix that Bernard Dudot, the father of the Renault V6 had a fascinating experience which says a lot about Senna the driver. After qualifying, the Brazilian

Eyewitness account from Gérard Ducarouge

The Lotus technical director was very well placed to speak about Ayrton Senna's incredible technical sensitivity: *"He was always looking for the ultimate in performance. For example, he could not cope with the idea of being one a half seconds up and leaving a new set of tyres unused in the pits. It was impossible to convince him to give it a rest. He could feel everything on the car. If he told us the dampers were not set up in the usual way and we told him they were without checking first, then we were in trouble! One day, we resurfaced some carbon brake discs, simply because we could not afford to fit a new pair each time, as the Lotus budget would not stretch to it. Ayrton was adamant he wanted new ones for qualifying, as was the case at McLaren, Williams and Ferrari. As far as we were concerned there was no difference and it was just so that he could feel the effect of the new carbon. The first thing he said after just one lap was "I'm not driving a car without new discs!" We got a ticking off. So in the end, we did as he asked, but given the cost, the bills were mounting up. And it's true that when it came to one click on a damper or a turn on an anti-roll bar, there was no fooling him. He was mad about the smallest detail and had incredible sensitivity."*

Archives: Gérard Ducarouge

• **39**_Elio de Angelis found it hard to accept the lightning superiority of his new team-mate and was soon destroyed by the Brazilian phenomenon.

● **40**_On 6th October 1985 at Brands Hatch for the European Grand Prix, Senna stunned the world with his extreme driving style; all except Keke Rosberg in the Williams who had a tyre punctured by the Lotus. The fuming Finn left the pits one lap down, just ahead of the Brazilian who was busy chasing Mansell in the lead. Keke later admitted he did all he could to help team-mate Nigel win!

explained his quick lap with such precision that the engineer was completely gobsmacked. He omitted nothing, remembering the engine temperatures in each sector, ditto the turbo pressure, the engine revs, the oil pressure and the gears for each part of the track. All of it had been taken on board at an average speed of 200 km/h on one of the most dangerous tracks. The great champions are all capable of doing this, but with Senna it reached a higher level. There was no real-time telemetry in those days, but when the data was downloaded from the car, the figures corresponded exactly to those Ayrton had given Dudot. The Frenchman felt the need to sit down!

At the end of the year, it was obvious that but for the endless mechanical failures, the Brazilian prodigy would have really been in the running for the championship title in what was only his second season in Formula 1. Ayrton had unveiled every facet of his incredible multi-talented being. Some of them just needed a bit of fine tuning, while some of the faults which irked his contemporaries would have to be rectified. Keke Rosberg was quick to brand Senna a "dangerous driver" when they had a heated clash at Brands Hatch. Michele Alboreto also had cause to be riled by the Brazilian virtuoso this year.

While some talked of danger, others simply admired the extreme commitment of a man for whom the words "give up" simply did not exist. Right from his earliest karting days, Ayrton

Senna's on track motivation was always very intense and in some people's opinion too extreme. It is true that he would only lift off the throttle on the rarest of occasions, but that was just his style, which combined going as quickly as possible on the perfect line. His overtaking moves were carried off with such skill that few drivers could hold him off. He made his move as quickly as possible without taking into account the reactions of the driver he was overtaking. This attitude meant the several rivals almost parked their cars to get out of the way when they saw the famous yellow helmet in their mirrors, but his method did have limitations, especially if he came up behind someone as stubborn as himself. His only real fault was an inability to admit to mistakes; an attitude which rubbed up some of his competitors the wrong way. Gerard Ducarouge's point of view was that "only mediocre drivers are dangerous."

When the driver market season got underway, Ayrton was naturally chased after in no uncertain terms. Bernie Ecclestone had just found out that Piquet was off to Williams for 1986 and he reckoned he could do to Warr, what Warr had done to the Toleman brothers the previous year. He invited Senna to travel with him in his personal jet and put all his cards on the table. But Ayrton had learnt his lesson from 1984 and was not prepared to relive the trauma which followed the news of his move to Lotus and politely turned down the offer from Formula 1's money man. On top of that, Peter

Designers: Gérard Ducarouge and Martin Ogilvie

Engine

Make/Type: Renault EF15C
Number of Cylinders/Configuration: V6 (Rear)
Capacity: 1494 cc
Bore/Stroke: 80.1 x 49.4 mm
Compression ratio: 7.5 : 1
Turbo(s): 2, Garrett
Maximum power: 850-900 hp (+ 1200 tests)
Maximum revs: 12000 rpm
Block material: Aluminium
Fuel/Oil: Elf
Sparking plugs: Champion
Injection: Bendix/Renault Sport
Valve gear: 4 OHC
Number of valves per cylinder: 4
Ignition: Renault Sport
Weight (without intercoolers): 140 kg

Transmission

Gearbox/Number of gears: Lotus (5/6)
Clutch: AP

Chassis

Type: Carbon monocoque
Suspensions: Wishbones, pullrods (Front and Rear)
Shock absorbers: Koni
Rim diameter: 13" (Front and Rear)
Rim width: 11.5" (Front) / 16.25" (Rear)
Tyres: Goodyear
Brakes: Brembo/SEP discs

Dimensions

Wheelbase: 2720 mm
Track: 1800 mm (Front) / 1620 mm (Rear)
Dry weight: 540 kg
Fuel capacity: 195 litres

Used all season.

Warr was not at all impressed with attempts to poach his driver and Ecclestone tip-toed away from the deal. In any case, the future at Ketteringham Hall looked brighter than at Chessington and Ayrton had total confidence in Gerard Ducarouge, who had become, if not quite a friend, then at least a confidant. Ayrton did not have many friends and most of those were Brazilian. Europe meant work to him and work ruled out any deep and meaningful friendships. Nevertheless, the relationship which the two men carved out between them during three years of working together, went much further than a simple polite working partnership.

Senna therefore embarked on the 1986 season with the same technical package, albeit revised and refined. The 98T was a simple evolution of its predecessor, with an ultra-light one piece carbon-fibre tub. The V6 turbo now had even more grunt, putting out 900 horsepower in race trim. For qualifying, the Viry-Chatillon engineers produced special engines which were only good for a handful of laps but delivered an unbelievable cavalry charge of 1300 horsepower! It would be the final year of madness in terms of these power figures which had been unimaginable only a few years earlier. It was reckoned that in private testing, Honda had managed to get 1500 horsepower out of a V6, achieving the magical 1000 brake horsepower per litre figure! In 1987, FISA introduced a turbo boost pressure restriction, before finally banning the turbo engines from 1989 onwards. For Senna's high-wire act this amount of power was manna from heaven. He took the most poles in 1986 (eight) and his death defying image was even more to the fore. As always after the season, Ayrton applied his cold analytical mind to the situation. He had definitely made that important leap by winning in Formula 1 and had make his mark in that new world right from his second season. But he also examined the state of play at Lotus. While it held plenty of promise on the technical front, there was not enough of it to go round, which meant that by his reckoning, the team did not have the funds to prepare two cars in the best way possible. That led to Senna mentioning his doubts when the team had to start hunting around for a team-mate for the Brazilian for 1986. The initial and generally popular choice was to go for the solid Englishman, Derek Warwick. But even though his qualities as a competent and aggressive fighter seemed to make him the ideal choice, Senna did not go along with it, even though Warwick had first hand knowledge of the Renault V6, having raced in the team of that name in 1984 and '85. But Senna was not about to give in. He wanted absolutely to win the world championship that year and was keen for the team to be totally focussed on his car. The English press was scandalised that Lotus did not take Warwick on board, reckoning that Ayrton had been frightened of an embarrassing showdown within the team. In retrospect, that argument did not hold water, as it is unlikely that Derek would have given the Brazilian much trouble. In the end, it was the young Johnny Dumfries who was the lucky recipient of the drive. A nice lad from an aristocratic family, he would, even more than Warwick, be there simply to make up the numbers and would not get in the way.

At the start of 1986, the Lotus 98T would make sparks fly. It usually qualified in the top half of the field and in the race, it hummed round with metronomic regularity. Ayrton came away from seven races with two wins, three podium finishes, one fifth and only one retirement due to mechanical failure. After the United States Grand Prix, he was leading the championship. And how! The sight of the black

and gold JPS tackling the Eau Rouge kink at Spa was something to see, as sparks flew before it hurtled up the climb to the Kemel straight. The Spa race saw sparks fly off the track as well, as it was at this point of the season that the opposition, led by Patrick Head, started to raise inquisitive eyebrows. The Williams technical director was clear on the subject, reckoning the car was illegal. He was convinced it had flexible bodywork which meant the ride height was adjustable thus creating illegal ground-effect. The folks at Lotus were delighted, because all this fuss meant the team was regarded as a real threat. It was certainly a situation which would have delighted Colin Chapman, who loved to provoke controversy. But the sound of protest grew louder and Gerard Ducarouge decided that enough was enough. He approached the governing body, suggesting they take the car apart after the next qualifying session. The car was simply set up very low for the final qualifying run and in fact became very difficult to drive as a consequence. As far as the Frenchman was concerned, the only "illegal" thing about it was the driver. He was the one who should have been disqualified on the grounds of being too magic!

Senna's two wins were delivered in different styles, but both reflected the enormous depth of talent he could call on when the chips were down. Leading on the new Jerez de la Frontera circuit in the second round of the championship, he did all he could to conserve his tyres, which had worn down to the canvas, before using all his skill to fight off the hard charging Nigel Mansell in the Williams. An old hand by now, Ayrton made his car very wide for the last few laps, before accelerating as hard as he could coming out of the final left hand

● **40**_ "I've won!"– "No, I have!" In 1986, at the new Jerez circuit, Senna and Mansell staged a photo finish.

hairpin before the main straight. The Englishman did the same and the two men crossed the line side by side. Mansell was convinced he had won and so was Senna. The timing beam found in favour of the Lotus by fourteen thousandths of a second! Two months later in Detroit, Senna had a puncture in the early stages and dropped down to eighth after pitting. Everyone had written off the Brazilian's chances, but he staged an amazing comeback, just as Alain Prost had done in Kyalami in 1982, before taking the lead at about two thirds distance. This victory on a street circuit with several traps for the unwary was to be the first of a string of wins conquered in the streets of Detroit, Phoenix and Monaco.

By now, everyone was talking about Ayrton Senna's chances of winning the title, but things were about to take a turn for the worse. A lurid high speed slide for the Lotus at the Paul Ricard circuit in the opening laps of the French Grand Prix was the start of the slippery slope. Senna was caught out by a patch of oil and could not keep the car on track. Then he only managed 27 laps of Brands Hatch before retiring with a seized gearbox. Thanks to a couple of second place finishes in Germany and Hungary, he was back in the race for the title, if not the lead. However, two further retirements in Austria and Italy meant he gave up any real hopes of becoming champion. There were only three races to go and he would have to be brilliant to stage a comeback. Two insufficient third places would destroy the young man's dream. Up against the powerful, reliable and relatively consistent Honda engine in the Williams, the Renault could match it in the power stakes, but was more fragile and

Chapter **9**

The Threshold

• **46**_A new look as Lotus changed its colours. Perfectionist as usual, Senna even got Syd Mosca, the Brazilian artist who had deisgned his helmet seven years earlier, to ensure that the yellow matched the new Lotus colour.

With hindsight, one could say that Senna made the mistake of staying one season too many with Lotus. In fact, he had no real alternative. Despite making lots of contacts, the doors did not open in the way he had hoped. Ron Dennis would have liked to get Senna, but he did not have the Honda engine. Senna would have liked to go to Williams which did have the Honda engine, but Piquet and Mansell were already there. Finally, Ferrari was not prepared to stretch to Senna's technical and financial demands. So Senna had to stay with Lotus, who had just signed up for the Honda V6.

Along with the much coveted engine, Ducarouge had come up with a technical package including an innovative suspension system. The 99T was fitted with revolutionary suspension, fitted with electronic sensors, which was known as "active." The general principal was that the slightest change in track surface was

recorded by an on-board computer which fed the information to the four corners of the car. In theory, it would provide a degree of comfort for the driver in a car whose ride height remained unaltered and could be tailored according to the demands of each circuit. In practice, it turned out to be far more complicated and that was the down side. Right from the first test sessions, the engineers realised they were up against amazingly complex electronics. Project leader Peter Wright felt that settings found for a particular circuit could then be used on similar tracks. However, the system was so sensitive that nothing worked as planned and the system had to be re-set each time out. The projected time saving had gone out the window.

Another problem that immediately raised its head was the fact the Honda V6 vibrated so badly that all the engine mounting points had to be strengthened. This did not stop one

mounting breaking away in the first round in Brazil, causing an oil leak, which forced Senna to retire. Putting aside this problem and a first lap retirement in Spa, provoked by an over eager Nigel Mansell, Ayrton experienced a very encouraging start to the 1987 season. As in the previous year, he was leading the championship after the United States Grand Prix in Detroit. He had taken two wins in a row, including his first at Monaco. These two races showcased the advantages of the active suspension on bumpy tracks. But everyone at Lotus had their doubts and Senna was very pessimistic about how things would work out on the fast circuits still to come.

Those fears were confirmed because although the Lotus-Honda finished pretty much all the remaining rounds, it was hardly ever in the fight for the win. It was handicapped by a less aerodynamic package than the Williams,

lacked top speed and used more fuel. Senna reckoned the team had concentrated so much on the active suspension that it had neglected the basics. The truth of that statement was visible from the fact that the "pole king" only started from the number one slot once, early in the season at Imola. Naturally, he showed a good turn of speed and was invariably on the first or second row. However, there was nearly always one or two Williams ahead of him. Ducarouge tried his best to tune the package, but the damage was done. The Lotus team's shortcomings were visible once again: a lack of funds compared with the other top teams, which meant the development programme suffered. Senna reminded Peter Warr that he had warned him about this at the start of the year, but the team boss was beginning to get fed up with being given lessons in economics by his driver.

• **47**_The first of six coronations in the Principality. Thanks to the active suspension, Ayrton took a relatively easy win in Monaco.

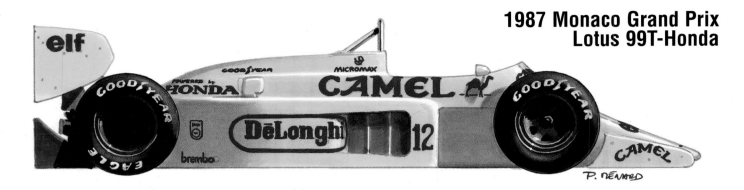

P. RÉNARD

Designers: Gérard Ducarouge and Martin Ogilvie

Engine

Make/Type: Honda RA 166-E and 167-G
Number of Cylinders/Configuration: V6 (Rear)
Capacity: 1500 cc
Bore/Stroke: not given
Compression ratio: not given
Turbo(s): 2, IHI
Maximum power: 900 - 1000 hp
Maximum revs: not given
Block material: Cast alloy
Fuel/Oil: Elf
Sparking plugs: NGK
Injection: Honda/PGM-F1
Valve gear: 4 OHC
Number of valves per cylinder: 4
Ignition: Honda
Weight (without intercoolers): not given

Transmission

Gearbox/Number of gears: Lotus (5/6)
Clutch: AP

Chassis

Type: Carbon monocoque
Suspension: Wishbones, pullrods (Front), Double wishbones, pushrods (Rear)
Shock absorbers: Lotus "Active Suspension"
Rim diameter: 13" (Front and Rear)
Rim width: 11.5" (Front) / 16" (Rear)
Tyres: Goodyear
Brakes: Brembo/SEP discs

Dimensions

Wheelbase: 2730 mm
Track: 1790 mm (Front) / 1640 mm (Rear)
Dry weight: 540 kg
Fuel capacity: 195 litres

Used all season. 166-E in Brazil, 167-G the rest of the season.

Relations between the two men began to deteriorate, with Ducarouge stuck in the middle as the referee. This time, Ayrton quickly realised he was in a sticky situation and decided to take the bull by the horns. He was in his fourth season of Formula 1 and it looked as though, yet again, the championship was going to slip from his grasp. There was no time to lose and so he contacted Ron Dennis.

Given how well McLaren was going for several years now, it was obvious to the Brazilian that he had to get himself a berth there. 1987 was not actually the best of years for the Marlboro backed team, given that Porsche had announced it was pulling out. But McLaren had still taken the Drivers' title for the past three years, with Lauda in 1984 and Prost in 1985 and '86. The Frenchman was setting the standard in

Formula 1; the most complete driver of his day. He was very charismatic and the team was built around him. Cohabiting with the Frenchman was the most enriching experience of Senna's life. First he would learn and then he would beat him. What better perspective than to become world champion using the same car as the best driver in the world? Discussions went on throughout the summer. Dennis revealed to Senna that he would have the V6 Honda for 1988, as the Japanese had grown tired of the deteriorating atmosphere within the Williams team between Piquet and Mansell. Pretty certain as to his future, Ayrton Senna broke his silence towards Peter Warr to announce he would not be driving for him the following year. Warr reacted by taking the initiative, announcing that Senna would be shown the door at the end of 1987.

● **48**_In Detroit, active suspension once again saw the Lotus cope well with the pavements and manhole covers of the street circuit. It was the last win.

Everything was now in place for Ayrton Senna to sign a contract, tying him to McLaren International for the next three years. Ayrton still had one plan up his sleeve. While in his heart he was relieved to be leaving Lotus, he was not keen on parting company with Gerard Ducarouge. He tried to persuade the Frenchman to follow him to McLaren, especially as Dennis had already made him an offer to join as technical director, with a very attractive package. But the engineer did not want to break his contract with Lotus and, as he admitted, did not really trust Dennis as a man. Ayrton therefore had to leave his engineer and confidant to his fate, in a team which was about to go through an agonising time, starting the following season.

The news was announced on the eve of the Italian Grand Prix: Ayrton Senna would drive for McLaren alongside Alain Prost in 1988. Marlboro had broken open its piggy bank to meet Ayrton's demands, the Brazilian now living a superstar lifestyle. He owned a big house in Esher in Surrey and he rented a flash apartment in Monaco, surrounded by sports stars and celebrities, all there because of the attractive taxation laws in the Principality. By now, he was also flying around in his own private jet. A few days before the Italian Grand Prix, Ron Dennis laid on a high class press reception for the world's media, to introduce his high class driver line-up. Prost and Senna mechanically trotted out the usual platitudes. Alain was pleased that the team was now boosted by a man whom everyone saw as a future world champion. For his part, Ayrton recognised that the double world champion's track record was edifying and worthy of respect, although he added that come the end of the season, the world champion would be the best of the two of them. It was a simple statement of intent. ■

Eyewitness account of Gérard Ducarouge

Was active suspension a step forward or a blind alley?
"I pushed hard to have it, but it was a very bad experience. To be totally honest, I was completely incapable of getting the system to work. There were two guys at Lotus who could deal with it, including an engineer on secondment from Cranfield university. He had designed active systems for fighter planes and these were then adapted for suspensions. I drove the famous Lotus Esprit fitted with this system and I thought it would allow a driver to drive a Formula 1 car in total comfort. But it was big and heavy and so we had to set about making it smaller. Then it worked. We won two grands prix and we had very few problems with it. I was terrified, because if there was a failure in the system, then the car had no suspension at all. We invested a lot in this system which meant we did a lot less work on the car as a whole.
Ayrton had never ending discussions with the engineers who controlled the software, but it was not his style. I have to say, he didn't like it as it was too complicated. It was a computer doing the work and he could not "translate" what it was doing. But he did love the comfort level it provided as he had very soft hands and was always getting blisters. He meticulously strapped his hands up with bandages. He would not let anyone help him with this, insisting on doing it all himself. It was a real ritual. And in Monaco, as soon as he stepped out of the cockpit, the first thing he showed us was his hands: no blisters!"

• **49**_Despite a few mid-season tweaks, the Lotus "active" was not a total success. Here in Portugal, where Ayrton finished a distant 7ᵗʰ, Gerard Ducarouge (bent down on left) and Osamu Goto, the Honda boss (standing in shorts) try to find an acceptable solution for the Brazilian, who was visibly tiring of the situation.

Chapter 10
The better of the two

This looked like being Senna's best ever season in Formula 1. He was now in the best structured team with the best performance on offer and he was driving alongside the best driver in the world, powered by the most powerful engine. The technical team was peerless, led by the magisterial Gordon Murray, McLaren's technical director since 1987, having worked for fourteen years with Brabham. Murray had guided designer Steve Nichols in his work on the new MP4/4, which was low, slim and nimble; everything that the 1986 Brabham BT55 was not, due largely to a lack of funds.

Right from the very first McLaren-Honda test session, a slight air of tension was palpable between the two drivers, even if on the surface everything was just fine between them. Prost kept a wary eye on his extremely punctilious

responded immediately and the Frenchman, realising he was beaten, decided to settle for second place. Aware of this, Ayrton then relaxed, but unforgivably lost concentration. His lap times were erratic and, with two laps remaining, the barriers at Portier corner reached out and bit him. He just had time to take his hands off the wheel to avoid injury to his wrists and piled into the barrier, in all senses of the phrase.

A few minutes later, while Alain could hardly believe he was standing on the top step of the podium, Ayrton was already back in his apartment, just a couple of hundred metres from where he retired. He was devastated, as he struggled to understand what he had done wrong. Was his strategy, as ever based on pure speed, bound to fail when up against Prost's uncanny race craft and intelligence? The fact was that the Frenchman now had a ten point lead in the championship after just three races. Then it hit him: his McLaren was a rocket and he had made the mistake of trying to drive it like a taxi over those last few miserable laps. He had never been the sort to count the pennies and he was not about to start now, not when he knew the title was there for the taking for the fastest driver. The next few races would show that the MP4/4 was in a league of its own; way ahead of

the opposition. The Ferraris were too thirsty, Lotus was not in the game and those now running normally aspirated engines were not in the hunt. The title would therefore be a showdown between the two McLaren employees. Ayrton was back on track, his confidence regained, having dug deep inside his psyche, while relying on his deep-seated belief in God. With a Bible always at hand, which he referred to every day, he felt ready to deal with the pressures and the crowds that followed him everywhere.

After the French Grand Prix, which marked the mid-point of the season, Prost led Senna by 15 points, although the Brazilian had four wins to the Frenchman's three. In France, Prost had even shown his team-mate that he could overtake "Senna-style," when he got him in the Beausset double right hander which he knew so well, as he slid past with the help of an uncooperative backmarker. But one week later, the British Grand Prix held in pouring rain, overturned the balance of power. Not only did Senna put on another demonstration of his mastery of the wet conditions, but Prost simply chose to pull out of the race, claiming his car was "undriveable". Senna had gained the psychological high ground. He did it again three

● **54**_A stylish performance at Silverstone brought more than just another win for Ayrton Senna. He had also seriously dented Prost's morale, as the Frenchman had pulled out of a race where he felt he had nothing to win.

• **55**_Ayrton savours the moment on the Spa podium. He has just taken his fourth consecutive win to lead the championship and bolster his chances of taking the title. Alain Prost seems resigned, while Thierry Boutsen, first of the normally-aspirated brigade for Benetton, congratulates his friend.

Eyewitness account from Gordon Murray

When he joined McLaren at the end of 1986, Gordon Murray was immediately seduced by Prost's qualities. Then, along came Senna and the technical director admits he was bowled over by running these two champions together:

"They were a gang! Fantastic. And it was a real challenge, because the two men did not really fit together. I had very strict rules for the drivers, with serious penalties. I did not want them to act separately, talking to engineers behind the trucks. I had to keep a close eye on them. But I loved my time with them. Getting them to work together was the reward. Even if you have two quick drivers, if they don't cooperate, you don't win all the races you should have won. And in 1988, we nearly won all of them! We had an extremely reliable car, a bit like the Brabham BT49, which I am really proud of. Senna and Prost; I was proud of them, even though they had two completely different and strong characters. Senna was much more cerebral than Prost, much more. He was always a few steps ahead of you and could see the next move perfectly clearly, like a chess player."

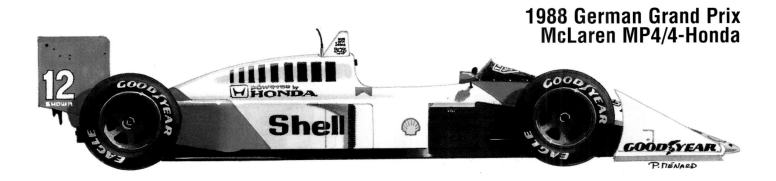

Designer: Steve Nichols

Engine

Make/Type: Honda RA 168-E
Number of Cylinders/Configuration: V6 (Rear)
Capacity: 1494 cc
Bore/Stroke: 79 x 50.8 mm
Compression ratio: 9.6 : 1
Turbo(s): 2, IHI
Maximum power: Around 650 hp
Maximum revs: 12500 rpm
Block material: Cast alloy
Fuel/Oil: Shell
Sparking plugs: NGK
Injection: Honda/PGM-F1
Injection: 4 OHC
Number of valves per cylinder: 4
Ignition: Honda
Weight (without intercoolers): 150 kg

Transmission

Gearbox/Number of gears: McLaren (6)
Clutch: AP

Chassis

Type: Carbon monocoque
Suspensions: Wishbones, pullrods (Front), Double wishbones, pushrods (Rear)
Shock absorbers: Showa
Rim diameter: 13" (Front and Rear)
Rim width: 11.5" (Front) / 16.3" (Rear)
Tyres: Goodyear
Brakes: Brembo/SEP discs

Dimensions

Wheelbase: 2875 mm
Track: 1824 mm (Front) / 1640 mm (Rear)
Dry weight: 540 kg
Fuel capacity: 150 litres

Used all season.

more times in Germany, Hungary and Belgium with three demonstrations of pure driving skill on the limit. The victory at Spa crucified the Frenchman. Just before the start, Prost had asked for his rear wing to be backed off to give him a bit more top speed on this fast flowing circuit. He made the better start, but the Brazilian was visibly quicker and swept past on the opening lap at the end of the long Kemel straight. The suspense was over and Senna spent the rest of the race enjoying a Sunday afternoon stroll to the flag, out on his own at the head of the field. From then on, Prost seemed resigned to his fate. Eleven of the sixteen rounds had been run and the incredible McLaren-Honda had won all of them. As the rules stated that not all results counted towards the championship, they worked against Prost's steady approach. Ayrton knew he could clinch the title at the very next round at Monza.

Beneath the Italian podium, the crowd was hysterical with delight: the Ferrari duo of Michele Alboreto and Gerhard Berger had triumphed and not one McLaren had made it to the flag! Prost retired with a very rare failure on the Honda V6. Senna was leading with a few laps to go, when he tangled with Jean-Louis Schlesser's Williams at the first chicane. The stand-in driver had moved as far off line as he could, but spun on the dirty side of the track. Senna took it calmly, accepting poor Schlesser's embarrassed apologies. Realistically, Ayrton felt the title had simply been delayed until Portugal or maybe Spain. It was now that Alain Prost, whom everyone including Ayrton felt was now a spent force, was about to prove that he was still a man to be reckoned with.

Maybe his morale had been boosted by his team-mate's failure. Maybe he felt that Honda had finally given him a better engine, having suspected the Japanese manufacturer of

favouring the Brazilian. Whatever the reason, the double world champion returned to sparkling form on the Iberian peninsula, winning at both Estoril and Jerez. These emphatic victories put him fair and square back in the race for the title. Senna seemed off colour, picking up just a few points, aware that his engine seemed to suffer from serious fuel consumption problems. But more than that, he felt his team-mate had got one over on him.

At the second start in Estoril, the race having been stopped because of an accident, Ayrton was caught napping by Alain, who had the inside line. He pulled alongside as they headed for the first corner, but realised he was being moved over towards the grass verge. The Brazilian gritted his teeth, kept going and took the lead. But next time round, Prost was definitely quicker and was up the Brazilian's exhausts, before once again trying to make the classic move down the inside. Senna then made a sudden move to the right, deliberately squeezing his rival against the pit wall at 280 km/h! The crowd leapt to its feet fearing the worst from this vicious attack. But this time, it was Prost who would not give way and he took the lead. After the race, the press massed around the McLaren motorhome to get the low-down on the latest internecine struggle. But they came away empty handed. Inside the bus, Ron Dennis had given his two men a severe dressing down, ordering them to cease hostilities. Obviously, Alain's ill-advised move and Ayrton's exaggerated response had been deliberate, but neither man criticised the other. This sort of intimidation was tacitly condoned in this battle of the titans of Formula 1, but it had not been seen for a long time. There were just two rounds remaining and although just one win would be enough for him to take the title, Ayrton's route was looking steeper than before.

When the green light came on for the start at Suzuka, he must have thought for a fraction of a second that the climb was now impossible. As the howling pack swarmed around him, poor Ayrton desperately tried to get his stalled engine to fire up. He managed it because of the downhill slope of the track.

•56_At Estoril, a reinvigorated Prost tries to intimidate his team-mate at the start. Payback came a lap later…and how!

92

He was 14th coming through the first corner, while Prost was already long gone in the lead. By the time he came past the pits at the end of the opening lap, he was already up to eighth! The V6 Honda was now working like a well-oiled watch and Ayrton dug deep to make up for the delay. He was incandescent and picked off those ahead of him, most of whom prudently moved out of the way and by lap 20 he was lying second. Just ahead of him, tantalisingly within his grasp was the other McLaren. As if some celestial ally had appeared on the scene to help out, a slight misty drizzle darkened some parts of the track. Senna concentrated on the shiny grey ribbon of tarmac and the red and white dot which grew bigger in his field of vision. Soon the word Marlboro, on the rear wing of the MP4/6 filled his sights. He sensed that Prost was in trouble. He knew the Frenchman was wary of a greasy track. The two champions came up behind a group of backmarkers and Ayrton sensed Prost hesitate for a split second. It was too late as the Brazilian moved across and slipped by. He overtook everyone and still he pressed on. As always, he wanted more. He even beat the lap record on lap 33. But then, as he realised it was raining, that he could be champion, but that he could also lose it all, as he had done at Monaco six months earlier, he realised he had to be careful and concentrate this time. As he passed the Race Director, he pointed at the sky, indicating the race should be stopped as conditions might get dangerous. Senna repeated the signalling every lap, but the race went full distance, with the chequered flag waved after 51 laps. Ayrton began bashing his helmet with his fists, waving at the crowd and again, banging his helmet. It was the best lap of honour of his life. Having left the car in parc ferme, he had a haggard expression as he was led towards the podium. Tears welled up in his eyes, as he thought of his family and all those who had helped him in his career. Then, finally on the top step of the podium, alongside Alain Prost and his mate Thierry Boutsen, he closed his eyes and thanked God. ∎

Chapter 11
Incomprehension

• **58**_One of the last photos of harmony and collaboration at McLaren: in the Interlagos pits at the start of the 1989 season, Alain Prost explains, Ayrton Senna listens, although seeming to doubt what he hears and Ron Dennis contemplates the strength in depth of his driver line-up.

ionel Froissart is one of the few journalists who knew both protagonists well in the hurricane which would rock Formula 1 over the two coming seasons and even cause the odd storm in the three after that. A few years back, he had this to say on the subject: "With the extreme rivalry between these two champions, it meant that even years later, people were either in the Prost camp or the Senna camp." Never in the history of Formula 1, which has seen all sorts of conflict, had there been anything as violent and radical. Going back over the years there have been several battles between competitors, but none fought with such intensity and rage. Both men were huge stars with a massive following and it was clear the sport wasn't big enough for both of them. The single force behind this terrible fight was the potential of these two men. They were the very best and each without the other would have enjoyed a long and boring reign of supremacy.

Everything seemed fine at the end of 1988: Ayrton had finally won the world championship and Alain had taken victory in the last race of the season in Australia, raising his personal tally to 35 wins. The two men had embraced on the Adelaide podium and apparently Prost was convinced that Senna would be a more relaxed character in 1989, having finally got the title he desired so much; the underlying sentiment being that the following year would be his. But the

Frenchman was soon forced to change his opinion. The Brazilian's will to win was going to be even stronger this year, as evidenced at the opening round in Rio. Caught on the hop at the start by Riccardo Patrese's Williams and the Ferrari of Gerhard Berger, Ayrton Senna was the meat in the sandwich as the trio braked for the first corner. Wanting to take the lead at any cost, he collided with the Ferrari and lost the nose of his McLaren MP4/5, necessitating a visit to the pits. The Brazilian fans thought his chances had gone out of the window and felt he was in any case to blame for the incident.

The technical stakes had changed radically that year, as the turbos had gone, so that Honda had produced a normally aspirated V10, with the intention of carrying on where the V6 turbo had left off. The MP4/5, designed by Neil Oatley, was an evolution of the previous year's car and the opposition feared another hegemony, as seen in 1988. McLaren would dominate the season once again and in no uncertain terms, but it was tougher than the previous year, in part because of the clash of personalities within the team.

For round two at Imola, the red and white cars monopolised the front row. Senna, who realised that he would not get far by pulling off stunts like the one in Brazil, suggested to Prost that they should not attack one another before the first braking area at Tosa. In other words, whoever got to the first corner first would have

the lead. Prost accepted the suggestion. Ayrton made a great start, followed by Alain who, as agreed, let him lead at Tosa. The race was then stopped because of Berger's fiery accident in the Ferrari. At the second start, Senna was caught out and Prost shot into the lead. This was not really what the Brazilian had in mind. He took the bit between his teeth to catch the other McLaren and passed it cleanly, before going into Tosa. From there, he went on to win the race, with Prost second. The Frenchman was furious as he stepped from his car and made that clear to the media microphones stuck under his nose. According to him, Senna had not respected their agreement about the start. The Brazilian clumsily

presented his own rather unconvincing case. As for Ron Dennis, he was beginning to worry how the rest of the championship was going to unfold, given its already stormy start. He tried to patch things up between them, asking Ayrton the culprit to apologise to Alain the victim. The guilty man did as he was told, even managing a small tear; doubtless the result of all the pressure which had built up on the back of the day's events.

If Senna had decided to "kill" Prost on the track one day, from this day on the Frenchman had vowed to get the upper hand psychologically over his adversary. He revealed what had gone on during their meeting to the French daily paper,

• **59**_A quick photographic recap of the Senna-Prost confrontation in 1989: it all began with a spat at Imola on 23rd April (top) and finished with this coming together at Suzuka on 22nd October (bottom).

"L'Equipe," even though it was supposed to have been a secret. He claimed that Senna had "collapsed." Ayrton was stunned by what he took to be a perfidious ignominy and warned the Frenchman that, from that moment on, he would never speak to him again. It meant that the two men invariably turned their backs on one another in the pits and the motor home and the necessary technical communication was always done through the intermediary of the McLaren and Honda engineers. Ayrton's motivation was always one of his strongest qualities, but this traumatic episode pushed it up a notch or two. Even more than before, his aggression at the wheel was now indestructable. His need to beat Prost was to see him take ever greater risks and he sometimes lost sight of reality. In 1989, although he won six races fair and square, his driving was occasionally erratic, rough and far from the perfection which he always sought. Nevertheless, he often proved capable of driving with his head, notably in Monaco, where he adjusted to gearbox problems after first dealing with his sworn enemy. In Mexico he won, by proving more adept at making the correct tyre choice than the man referred to as "The Professor" because of his tactical skills. Spa turned into another festival in the rain for him and he was rightly regarded as the natural

successor to Jim Clark on the Ardennes rollercoaster. Senna was still the brilliant driver, terrifying in his mastery of the one lap virtuoso performance to take pole and admired by spectators around the world. However, he became less and less serene as the 1989 season progressed.

The situation within the McLaren team was developing into an abscess which was only lanced when Alain Prost announced at the French Grand Prix that he was leaving the team at the end of the year. Ayrton seemed immune to this declaration. Nothing had changed for him and the enemy was still the same. Recent technical problems in the United States and Canada meant he was not willing to back off. He had to continue to fight and use any opportunity to get one over on Prost. This exponential obsession forced him into making errors which would cost him dear come the end of the season. In England, he got ahead of Prost, but soon ran into problems changing gear. Determined not to lose a place, he fought with his gear lever until the inevitable error on lap 11, which sent him spinning off into the gravel trap. In Monza, he spun when his engine seized. Totally immersed in the battle for the lead, Ayrton had forgotten to activate the Honda V10's emergency lubrication system. At Estoril, he was caught out by a

• **60**_Honda and Senna – a great love affair. The Japanese constructor celebrated its 50th Grand Prix win at Spa-Francorchamps. The Brazilian knew he owed the bulk of his F1 wins to the impressive skills of his Japanese partners.

disfunctional Mansell. The Englishman had been black flagged and Senna should have let the stubborn moustachioed one pass, knowing he would have to stop soon. At the final round in Adelaide, he wanted to show that even a torrential downpour could not daunt his driving skill in the very worst conditions. He ended up spearing the back of Martin Brundle's Brabham, simply because the visibility was virtually zero. It was fuel for those who thought he was a danger to all. They were examples of his incomprehension, which was unusual for a man who knew better than most the meaning of the word "race." And of course there was Suzuka.

The penultimate race of the championship, the Japanese Grand Prix, was one of two last chances for Ayrton to catch up with Prost in the points. If he failed, the title would automatically go to the Frenchman. The tension between the two divas was huge. Prost told the press that he'd had enough of Senna's dangerous on-track moves and there would be no quarter given. He meant there would be no opening of any doors in the event of an overtaking movement, after he had been a bit too compliant in the recent past. The Brazilian did not take the threat on board. Enclosed in his shell, he would do the same as always.

Ayrton was surprised as the lights went on very quickly and he could see Alain charging off ahead of him. Already angry with himself for being caught out so stupidly, he took it out on his car which did not seem up to the job of of catching Prost's McLaren which seemed better balanced. Well aware that second place was worthless to him, he charged around the

magnificent Japanese track lapping as fast as he could. As had happened the previous year, he began to catch up with Prost. It took him forty laps to close on the leader and attempt to push him into a mistake. It was proving difficult as the McLaren no. 2 had a better aerodynamic configuration and the tight nature of the track made overtaking difficult. On lap 47 of 53, Senna went for a do or die effort under braking for the final Casio chicane. He went down the inside, moving into the pit lane entry. Prost had strategically positioned himself in the middle of the track. Senna nudged his McLaren towards the kerb when he noticed his team-mate darting to the right, cutting him off. He had ignored Prost's warning and now the Frenchman had slammed the door in his face.

The two cars finished up with their wheels interlocked in the chicane escape road. Ayrton looked across and gave Alain an ironic thumbs up. The Frenchman ignored him, got out of his car and headed for race control where the French president of FISA, Jean-Marie Balestre was waiting for him. Ayrton got the marshals to push him down the escape road and managed to get his engine running again. He completed the lap, before pitting to change the nose of his car. He emerged a minute later with the firm intention of taking the lead off the Benetton of Alessandro Nannini, whose lead was just a few seconds. Three laps later, more determined than ever, he pulled off the same move at the chicane and the likeable Sandro, deciding that discretion was the better part of the valour, let Ayrton Senna, the king of Japan, slide through to win the race. After the finish, he was disqualified, with the win

• 61_The 1989 Portuguese Grand Prix was a miserable event for Senna. Second behind Gerhard Berger (Ferrari no. 28), he was stupidly collected by Nigel Mansell (no. 27) who had already been excluded. Above all, he missed out on the opportunity to finish ahead of Prost (no. 2) who picked up the six points for second place.

Designer: Neil Oatley

Engine
Make/Type: Honda RA 109-E
Number of Cylinders/Configuration: V10 (Rear)
Capacity: 3490 cc
Bore/Stroke: 92 x 52.5 mm
Compression ratio: not given
Maximum power: 675 hp
Maximum revs: 13000 rmp
Block material: Aluminium
Fuel/Oil: Shell
Sparking plugs: NGK
Injection: Honda/PGM-F1
Valve gear: 4 OHC
Number of valves per cylinder: 4
Ignition: Honda
Weight: not given

Transmission
Gearbox/Number of gears: McLaren (6)
Clutch: AP

Chassis
Type: Carbon monocoque
Suspensions: Wishbones, pullrods (Front), Double wishbones, pushrods (Rear)
Shock absorbers: Showa
Rim diameter: 13" (Front and Rear)
Rim diameter: 12" (Front) / 16.3" (Rear)
Tyres: Goodyear
Brakes: Brembo/SEP discs

Dimensions
Wheelbase: 2896 mm
Track: 1820 mm (Front) / 1670 mm (Rear)
Dry weight: 500 kg
Fuel capacity: not given

Used all season.

going to Nannini, for three main reasons: 1) He had crossed into the pit lane entry which is not really part of the track, 2) he received external help to get going again and 3) he had cut the chicane to get back on track.

Ayrton was even more upset as he realised that the FISA president was behind it all. That was confirmed when a few days later, FISA stung him with a one hundred thousand dollar fine and a sixth month suspended race ban for "dangerous driving." This time, Ron Dennis got involved and asked for the race result to be suspended pending an appeal. This amazing situation had never been seen before in Formula 1, with a team owner defending one of his drivers against the other. It threw a cloud over a sport which would have liked to maintain an image of fair play. Many people, in the pro-Prost and pro-Senna camps reckoned they were disillusioned by the deleterious atmosphere which had descended on

Formula 1. For his part, Senna accused Jean-Marie Balestre of "having manipulated the championship in favour of Prost." The president had not exactly distinguished himself when it came to the finesse of his decision making. Senna said he would retire from racing if he was branded a hooligan on the track. He was visibly upset by all the accusations.

Ayrton Senna was not blameless in the affair and neither was Prost, but one thing was certain, the Brazilian's anguish was sincere. His extreme commitment certainly did not meet with universal approval, but that was his style and he could not conceive of driving like... Prost for example. Racing for points was just not in his psyche. He had to go as quickly as possible all the time. But this year, he fell into a trap set out by his team-mate and the trap had closed. It would take a good winter in the Brazilian sun to rediscover some serenity.

His break was seriously interrupted by a festering Jean-Marie Balestre who kept pushing for an apology for his public declarations. The tawdry affair dragged on as the all-powerful president threatened not to give the Brazilian a super-license for 1990. A concerned Ron Dennis begged Ayrton to apologise to avoid the worst.

The apology finally came but with bad blood. Dennis paid the fine and Balestre then wished Senna "*good luck for the championship!*" This ultimate insult was locked away in the Brazilian's memory banks and he would know when the time was right to bring it out again. ■

● **62**_A week after the Estoril debacle, Ayrton drove aggressively to his sixth win of the 1989 season. It was a job well done, but the hardest part now awaited him. He had to win in Suzuka and Adelaide to have any hope of taking the title.

● **63**_Japanese drama. Ayrton Senna drove like a man possessed on the challenging Suzuka circuit to catch up with his rival. A few laps later, at this same chicane, the game was over.

Chapter 12

A bitter revenge

• **64**_On lap 35 of 72 of the opening round of the 1990 season in Phoenix, Ayrton Senna took two bites of the cherry to move the humble Tyrrell, driven by astounding newcomer Jean Alesi out of the way. Ayrton later heaped praise on the Frenchman for his great showing.

Senna prepared to tackle this new season in what was manifestly the same frame of mind as the previous year. His will win to win had not wavered in the light of the events of 1989. He won the first event easily in the streets of Phoenix in the United States, but pointedly refused to shake Alain Prost's hand in the paddock. He still needed time to see how things would shake out this year.

Alain had left McLaren to join Scuderia Ferrari and his replacement, Gerhard Berger, suited Ayrton down to the ground. He was quick if a trifle inconsistent in terms of effort. Gordon Murray had left Formula 1 to concentrate on the McLaren F1 GT car and Neil Oatley was now technical director. The MP4/5B was, as its code name indicated, a simple evolution of the MP4/5. That would cause a few problems in the course of the year.

The season got underway in a shower of champagne for Senna with three wins from five starts. At Imola, he had been unable to defend first place because a wheel rim was damaged by a stone and in Interlagos, his chronic bad luck in Brazil lost him an almost certain victory. Other than that, things were looking good. At Interlagos, he had the measure of all his rivals.

Senna was preparing to lap Nakajima's Tyrrell, but the Japanese driver got out of shape and clipped the McLaren, so Senna was forced to pit for a new nose. He rejoined third and that's where he stayed to the flag, while Prost took his fortieth win at the wheel of his Ferrari. Ayrton would have preferred a more triumphal return to his home town of São Paulo at the new Interlagos circuit. On top of that, the disastrous economic situation in the country and an ill-timed visit from Jean-Marie Balestre only served to make the weekend even blacker.

Then came the summer and some difficult races. Alain Prost took three straight wins to lead the championship as the teams left Silverstone after the British Grand Prix. Ayrton did not hold back from telling Ron Dennis and Honda project leader Osamu Goto what he thought of it all. The McLaren chassis had progressed less than the Ferrari's and the Honda V10 lacked punch. The Paulista had the wherewithal to make them sit up and take notice and make progress, as at that time, he was renegotiating his contract for 1991 and was looking for solid technical guarantees or else. It had the desired effect and the Brazilian took charge once again at a crucial time in the championship, with three important wins at

● **65**_For the third time in his career, Ayrton raised the winner's trophy on the "tres chic" podium at Monaco. He would repeat this gesture a further three times.

Hockenheim, on his favourite track of Spa, where he was once again head and shoulders above the rest and at Monza, where he was untouchable. With a second place in Hungary, he had made a colossal comeback. After Italy, he was comfortably in the lead with a good cushion to fall back on, whereas Prost had it all to do.

Paradoxically, in a season which started with Ayrton in a win at all costs frame of mind, he was to start changing his attitude. He learnt to make do with podium finishes in France and England, without trying to win at all costs, as he did in the past, even when he did not have the wherewithal to do it. His driving style was smoother but no less effective as could be seen at Monaco and Spa. Senna seemed to possess inner calm during the post race press conference in Monza, sitting next to Alain Prost who had come second. As had become the custom, the two men never looked at one another as the two giants of the sport downloaded their thoughts on the race. It was the usual scenario until a brave journalist tossed in a hand grenade. He pointed out that they were here in this temple of speed, they had put on a great show and maybe the time had come to bury the hatchet, forget the past and make the peace. The room went quiet, before Prost said that, if Ayrton agreed, he could see nothing to stop it. Ayrton was very nervous and when it was his turn, explained that he would never forget what had happened, but if the move was sincere then he would go along with it. Alain then got up and held out his hand. Ayrton looked him deep in the eyes, hesitated for a moment and shook the proffered hand. The news spread through the paddock: they're talking again! One and a half months later another grenade, more serious this time would end this precarious and somewhat forced ceasefire.Qualifying for the Japanese Grand Prix was as tense as one could imagine, given the championship situation at the end of such a closely fought season. Prost knew he had to win to keep his championship chances alive in Australia. Senna was well aware that if his rival retired in one of these two races, he would be

● **66**_At the Hungaroring, Senna was heavily criticised for harpooning poor Sandro Nannini (behind in the Benetton). The Italian had passed the Brazilian who simply barged him off the track in cavalier fashion with a heavy handed passing move. As usual, the Brazilian denied all charges of wrong doing.

champion. For some incomprehensible reason, pole at Suzuka was on the right side of the track, the dirty side where there was less grip. Ayrton complained about it from the first day of the meeting, supported by Alain. No answer was forthcoming and it was in an increasingly bad mood that Ayrton took his ninth pole of the season, 25 hundredths of a second ahead of Alain Prost. In the Sunday morning driver briefing, the organisers confirmed that pole would stay where it was, that the pit lane entry prior to the Casio chicane could not be used for overtaking and that anyone sliding off into the escape road would be allowed to rejoin the circuit. You might as well have put a lit match to a powder keg!

The Brazilian showed his fury by storming out of the meeting. As far as he was concerned,

all this was done by the organisers to favour Prost. He knew the Ferrari had made enormous progress in the latter part of the season and that if he ended up behind it at the first corner, he would never see it again. His paranoia pushed him to make a decision which would have serious consequences.

At the start, the Ferrari logically shot into the lead, while the McLaren spun its wheels on the dirt. Gripping the steering wheel hard, Senna extracted everything from the Honda V10 and caught Prost as they approached the first corner, which is taken at around 240 km/h. He never lifted off and headed for the mouse trap which had begun to close. His front wheel sent the Ferrari back wing flying and Prost spun off into the gravel, followed by the McLaren which was

P. MÉNARD

Designer: Neil Oatley

Engine
Make/Type: Honda RA 100-E
Number of Cylinders/Configuration: V10 (Rear)
Capacity: 3498 cc
Bore/Stroke: not given
Compression ratio: not given
Maximum power: 690 hp
Maximum revs: 13000 rpm
Block material: Aluminium
Fuel/Oil: Shell
Sparking plugs: NGK
Injection: Honda/PGM-F1
Valve gear: 4 OHC
Number of valves per cylinder: 4
Allumage: Honda
Weight: 150 kg

Transmission
Gearbox/Number of gears: McLaren (6)
Clutch: AP

Chassis
Type: Carbon monocoque
Suspensions: Wishbones, pullrods (Front), Double wishbones, pushrods (Rear)
Shock absorbers: Bilstein
Rim diameter: 13" (Front and Rear)
Rim width: 11.5" (Front) / 16.3" (Rear)
Tyres: Goodyear
Brakes: Brembo discs

Dimensions
Wheelbase: 2950 mm
Track: 1800 mm (Front) / 1650 mm (Rear)
Dry weight: 500 kg
Fuel capacity: 220 litres

Used all season.

also damaged. It mattered little as Ayrton Senna had just taken his second world title.

As he walked back down the length of the pits, Ayrton was smiling, waving at well-wishers in the crowd and accepting the congratulations of his team. Then news filtered through about Prost's view of things. He accused the Brazilian of attempted murder, calling him a crazy fanatic. Senna swept away the Frenchman's words, saying he was a whiner and treated the whole affair with disdain. What he was unaware of was that, even amongst his closest supporters, the incident had not gone down well. Journalists pointed out that there was no way his move would have worked and that he had succumbed to inadmissible feelings of hate. He was shown photos of the incident and asked for the real story. He denied it all. This gesture had tarnished

a championship which, in other respects, was perfectly well deserved at the end of an exemplary season, but for this enormous error of judgement seen as sordid revenge. He faced a barrage of questions and was criticised from all sides, notably by Jackie Stewart who lectured him live on Australian television. Senna, fed up with the former champion's school masterly ways, sent him packing without standing on ceremony. The truth finally emerged a year later, again at Suzuka, when the Brazilian took his third title. Senna admitted he had deliberately driven Prost off the road in 1990. He explained that he did it to get at Jean-Marie Balestre through Prost. He wanted to get his own back for everything the former FISA president had put him through. It was easier for Ayrton to do it at this stage, as Balestre had been replaced by Max Mosley. ■

• **67**_At the start of the Italian Grand Prix, Senna charges off in the lead, while team-mate Gerhard Berger tries to contain Alain Prost in the Ferrari. In this role, Gerhard was Ayrton's model understudy.

• **68 and 69**_It has all just happened at the first corner of the 1990 Japanese Grand Prix. The wrecks of the Ferrari no. 1 and the McLaren no. 27 lie in the gravel trap, while their drivers head back to the pits without a glance, one in anger, the other savouring his revenge.

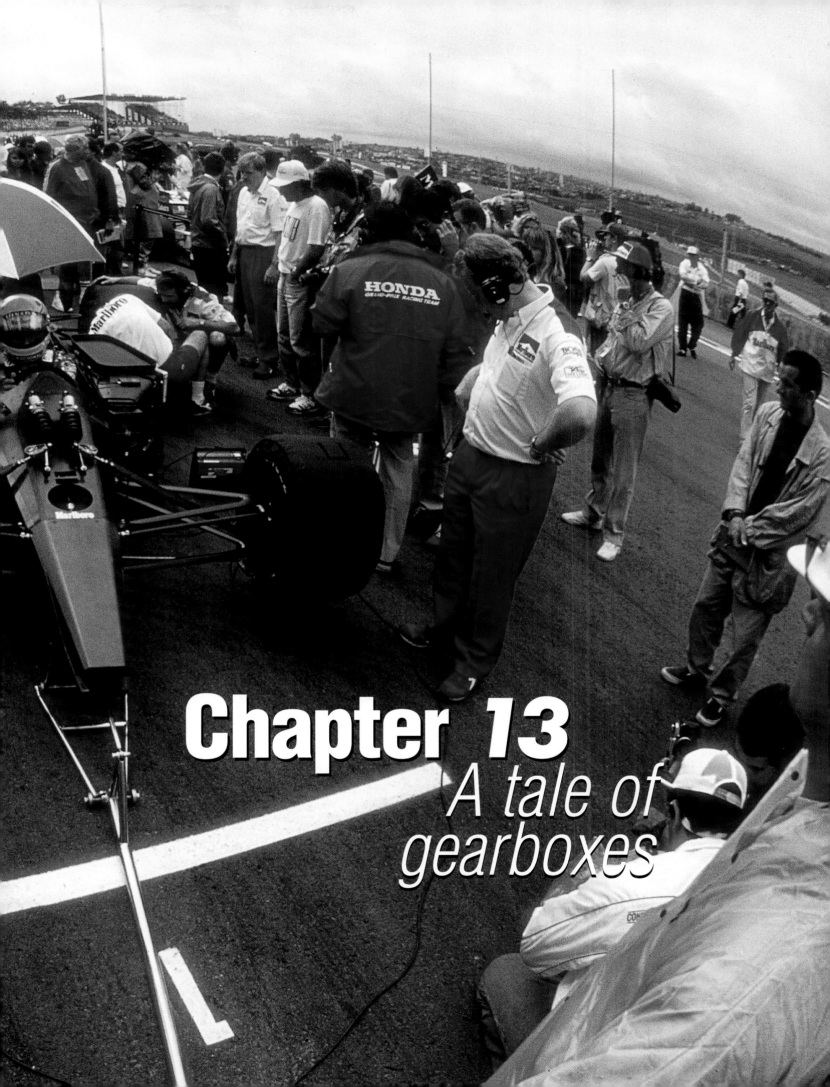

Chapter 13
A tale of gearboxes

"A memorable race"

Brazilian Grand Prix
24th March 1991

At the end of qualifying on Saturday 23rd March 1991, the grandstands of the Autodromo Jose Carlos Pace echoed to the deafening roar of thousands of fans cheering in delight: Ayrton Senna, the hero of São Paulo, had just taken pole position for his home Grand Prix. He had already won a fortnight earlier in the United States, at the first round of the world championship and the fact the double world champion was on great form made him the outright favourite for this race. Nevertheless, Senna was careful to play down his chances when quizzed by journalists, no doubt aware of his track record at home since he first took part in a Brazilian Grand Prix back in 1984.

Like all sportsmen, Senna always got a lift from performing on home turf. Whether in Rio or Interlagos, the crowd invariably almost literally pushed him towards victory. But no matter how often he looked like winning, fate always intervened. Bad luck, mechanical woes or the weather had robbed him of the chance to salute his fans from the top of the podium and the best he had managed was a second place in 1986, when he finished behind the "other" Brazilian, Nelson Piquet. He finished third the previous year, when a collision with Nakajima robbed him of almost certain victory. This afternoon's pole was his fifth, proving that he was a notch above the opposition in terms of pure speed. Over the past few years, along with the amazing Honda V10, the McLaren team had become a redoubtable winning machine, taking Senna to the world title twice and this year's MP4 car, very much built around him, looked ready to do it again. However, Ayrton still had his doubts.

He took an easy win in Phoenix two weeks earlier, in the face of very little opposition, but here he felt there was a real danger. The Ferraris might have been off the pace, but the Williams of Nigel Mansell and Riccardo Patrese now had an additional weapon in the shape of a type of semi-automatic gearbox and they looked to pose a threat. For no obvious reason, McLaren seemed to be lagging behind and Senna still had to make do with an old-fashioned gear lever! Towards the end of this session, the two Williams were quickest and the local boy made a last minute decision before going for one more attempt at snatching pole. He got the mechanics to reduce the angle of attack on the front wing, in order to pick up more straightline speed. The pay off of course was that he now had less downforce in the corners and had to get used to the feel of the car in this new trim. All the great drivers are adept at rapidly assessing the effects of such changes and adapting their driving style accordingly. But none of them ever came up to Ayrton's standard in this respect.

Senna went on to triumph and stand on the top step of the podium, on Sunday 24th March 1991. He showered himself copiously and at length with champagne. He savoured every drop of happiness and delight. A glance at the lap chart for the race shows that McLaren no. 1 led from start to finish. Another easy win then? Appearances and figures can be very deceptive as it was in fact a raw and very painful afternoon.

Everything went according to plan for the first half of the race. Ayrton made an impeccable start to lead and although he had not left the Williams duo for dead, he did have a comfortable margin. Mansell was the most aggressive of his pursuers and did occasionally close up to the Brazilian, who was trying to save his tyres as much as possible and after the pit stops he was reassured to find he was still in the lead. Not only that, but the Englishman needed a further visit to the pits because of a slow puncture. Senna now led Mansell by thirty five seconds, enough to get the samba bands in the grandstands to hit top gear in the sound stakes.

But the rhythms slowed and an agonised silence swept through the crowd. The McLaren appeared to be in difficulty and the Williams was closing in. The crowd was right behind the

Brazilian champion, but the reality of the situation was clear for all to see. There were still around fifteen laps to go and quite clearly, Senna the fighter was about to be beaten without being able to put up a fight. Then suddenly, Lady Luck, who had not been much use to him here in the past, decided to intervene. Mansell spun like a top because of a problem with the automatic gearbox and the impatient Englishman gave his transmission a real pasting in his hurry to get going again.

Ayrton was still not out of danger however. With ten laps to go, he no longer had 2nd or 4th gear and, sensing that the gearbox was about to fail completely, Senna never changed gear again that afternoon. Riccardo Patrese had been

running around forty seconds behind the McLaren and when he could see that the McLaren was lame, he closed in at around four seconds per lap! With seven laps to go, Senna's gearbox was stuck in sixth and he was on auto-pilot, totally exhausted. He had to brake much harder than usual to slow the car which no longer had the benefit of engine braking, which was usually a considerable force given that the 700 horsepower V10 had plenty of torque. He had to fight the steering wheel as the front end of the car now wanted to run wide at every corner. Once again, fate stepped in and lent a hand. In theory, Patrese would have passed the stricken McLaren in the closing stages, but he too was having gearbox worries and, having seen

McLaren MP4/6-Honda
1991 Brazilian Grand Prix

P. MÉNARD

Designer: Neil Oatley

Engine
Make/Type: Honda RA 121-E
Number of Cylinders/Configuration: V12 (Rear)
Capacity: 3493 cc
Bore/Stroke: not given
Compression ratio: not given
Maximum power: 710 hp
Maximum revs: 13000 rpm
Block material: Aluminium
Fuel/Oil: Shell
Sparking plugs: NGK
Injection: Honda
Valve gear: 4 OHC
Number of valves per cylinder: 4
Ignition: Honda
Weight: not given

Transmission
Gearbox/Number of gears: McLaren (6)
Clutch: not given

Chassis
Type: Carbon monocoque
Suspensions: wishbones, pushrods (Front and Rear)
Shock absorbers: Showa
Rim diameter: 13" (Front and Rear)
Rim width: 12" (Front) / 16.3" (Rear)
Tyres: Goodyear
Brakes: Brembo

Dimensions
Wheelbase: 2972 mm
Track: 1824 mm (Front) / 1679 mm (Rear)
Dry weight: 505 kg
Fuel capacity: 220 litres

Used all season.

Mansell caught out by the same problem, he decided to settle for a safe second place without putting his equipment under too much pressure. A few drops of rain started to fall right towards the end of the race, just to give the Brazilian something else to worry about, but he brushed these thoughts aside as the team hung out the "1 lap" board. As it took the chequered flag, the red and white car spluttered to a halt opposite the pits with its engine stalled.

The McLaren mechanics had to be very careful and patient as they rushed to revive their heroic driver and get him out of the cockpit. Interlagos had turned into one big party and the sound of samba exploded after the nail biting suspense and tension of one and a half hours of racing. Ayrton emerged slowly from the abyss and every one of his limbs ached with the pain, but the joy which radiated from him did not give a damn about his paralysed muscles. He was at home and he had finally won!

Ayrton Senna once again experienced the joy of winning in Interlagos in 1993, in a race characterised by a typical Paulista downpour. This time, even the gods were on his side, adding to the thrill of winning. Having spent the Eighties crossing the path of black cats in Rio, Ayrton seemed to have finally crushed them in São Paulo, the place where he grew up. And it was here that he would make his final journey in May 1994. ■

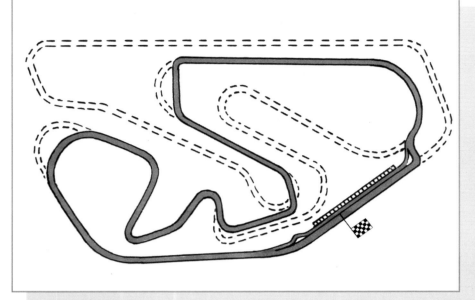

INTERLAGOS CIRCUIT
Permanent circuit
4.325 km / 2.688 miles

Situated in a suburb of São Paulo, the circuit was created after the second world war and was renovated at the end of the Sixties. Brazil then started lobbying for a Formula 1 Grand Prix and needed a circuit built to the required standard. Interlagos was it. The first Grand Prix was held in 1972, but did not count towards the world championship. That happened the following year and it rapidly became a major event for drivers and spectators alike. Emerson Fittipaldi, Brazil's first motor racing hero, won in 1973 and 1974 amid scenes of much excitement. Then it was Carlos Pace's turn in 1975. The young man had a glittering future ahead of him, when, along with the pilot, he

was killed in a helicopter crash in 1977. Since then, the circuit was named in his honour. Back then the track was 7.960 km long and resembled a tangled strand of spaghetti, running around some small lakes. Its most striking characteristic was that, unlike most tracks it ran anti-clockwise, which could cause neck problems for the drivers. It swept up and down with constant radius corners and long straights. Interlagos was dropped from the calendar at the end of the Seventies and over the years, the surface deteriorated, looking more like corrugated iron than anything else and the local authority ran out of money to maintain it.

The Rio-Jacarepagua track picked up the baton in 1981 after a trial run in 1978. It was there that Ayrton made his Formula 1 debut in front of a home crowd. After Fittipaldi, Pace and now Piquet, the young Paulista wanted to write his name on the Brazilian roll of honour. He would have to wait seven years.

Interlagos regained the Grand Prix in 1990. The layout had changed completely and its length reduced almost by half. A quick downhill "S", designed in consultation with Senna did a good job of linking the pit straight to the old Curva del Sol, to rejoin the track in the opposite direction. The site's natural character had been maintained and Ayrton was delighted to be back here and to win, because when all was said and done, Jacarepagua was only the circuit of his sworn enemy, the "Carioca" Nelson Piquet.

_SENNA AND THE BRAZILIAN GRAND PRIX

YEAR	CIRCUIT	QUALIFYING	RESULT	CAR
1984	Rio-Jacarepaguà	16th	Retired (turbo)	Toleman-Hart
1985	Rio-Jacarepaguà	4th	Retired (electrics)	Lotus-Renault
1986	Rio-Jacarepaguà	**Pole Position**	2nd	Lotus-Renault
1987	Rio-Jacarepaguà	3rd	Retired (engine seized)	Lotus-Honda
1988	Rio-Jacarepaguà.	**Pole Position**	Retired (black flagged)	McLaren-Honda
1989	Rio-Jacarepaguà	**Pole Position**	11th	McLaren-Honda
1990	Interlagos	**Pole Position**	3rd	McLaren-Honda
1991	Interlagos	**Pole Position**	**1st**	McLaren-Honda
1992	Interlagos	3rd	Retired (electrics)	McLaren-Honda
1993	Interlagos	3rd	**1st**	McLaren-Ford
1994	Interlagos	**Pole Position**	Retired (spin)	Williams-Renault

1. **Senna** 1:16.392
2. Patrese 1:16.775
3. Mansell 1:16.843
4. Berger 1:17.471
5. Alesi 1:17.601
6. Prost 1:17.739
7. Piquet 1:18.577
8. Gugelmin 1:18.664
9. Modena 1:18.847
10. Gachot 1:18.882
11. Bernard 1:19.291
12. Pirro 1:19.305
13. De Cesaris 1:19.339
14. Moreno 1:19.360
15. Capelli 1:19.517
16. Nakajima 1:19.546
17. Suzuki 1:19.832
18. Boutsen 1:19.868
19. Lehto 1:19.954
20. Martini 1:20.175
21. Morbidelli 1:20.502
22. Häkkinen 1:20.611
23. Comas 1:21.168
24. Tarquini 1:21.219
25. Blundell 1:21.230
26. Brundle 1:21.280

Lap chart

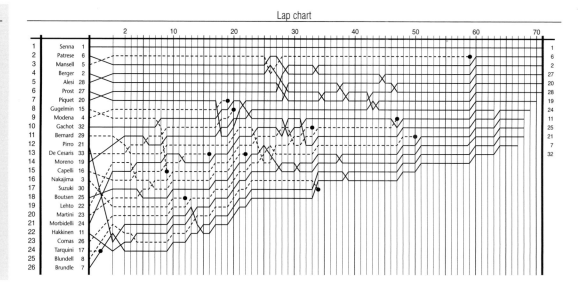

RESULTS - 71 race laps for 307.075 km

Pos	Driver	Car	Time/Gap
1.	Senna	McLaren-Honda	1:38:28.128 / 187.110 km/h
2.	Patrese	Williams-Renault	+ 2.991
3.	Berger	McLaren-Honda	+ 5.416
4.	Prost	Ferrari	+ 19.369
5.	Piquet	Benetton-Ford	+ 21.960
6.	Alesi	Ferrari	+ 23.641
7.	Moreno	Benetton-Ford	+ 1 lap
8.	Morbidelli	Minardi-Ferrari	+ 2 laps
9.	Häkkinen	Lotus-Judd	+ 3 laps
10.	Boutsen	Ligier-Lamborghini	+ 3 laps
11.	Pirro	Dallara-Judd	+ 3 laps
12.	Brundle	Brabham-Yamaha	+ 4 laps
13.	Gachot	Jordan-Ford	64 Ran out of fuel

RETIREMENTS

Driver	Car	Lap	Reason
Mansell	Williams-Renault	60	Transmission
Comas	Ligier-Lamborghini	51	Damaged car on kerb
Martini	Minardi-Ferrari	48	Accident
Blundell	Brabham-Yamaha	35	Engine
Bernard	Lola-Ford	34	Engine fire
Lehto	Dallara-Judd	23	Alternator
De Cesaris	Jordan-Ford	21	Accident
Modena	Tyrrell-Honda	20	Gearbox
Capelli	Leyton House-Ilmor	17	Transmission
Nakajima	Tyrrell-Honda	13	Accident
Gugelmin	Leyton House-Ilmor	10	Retired hurt
Tarquini	AGS-Ford	1	Accident
Suzuki	Larrousse-Ford	0	Engine

FASTEST RACE LAP

Driver	Car	Lap	Time
Mansell	Williams-Renault	35	1:20.436 / 193.570 km/h

● **71**_On the Interlagos podium: a happy Ayrton despite the pain of exhaustion. With a final effort, the son of São Paulo managed to hoist the cup to wave at his fans screaming for joy in the grandstands.

Chapter 14
The tryptich

● **72**_A sensational start to the 1991 season for Ayrton Senna: he won the first four grands prix (here at Monaco, ahead of an unexpected Stefano Modena in a Tyrrell) and was the firm favourite for the title. As he stepped out of the car, the Brazilian silenced those who said it was in the bag, saying life was about to get difficult. He was proved right!

Ayrton Senna was about to embark on his fourth season with McLaren. He now felt at home in the English team which was remarkably organised and perpetually in search of perfection. There was total osmosis with Ron Dennis in terms of their aims and the team's modus operandi conformed exactly with his own degree of perfectionism. His relationship with Gerhard Berger was now one of friendship. The laid-back Austrian had been completely out-paced on the track by the Brazilian tyrant, but this had no effect on the way they got on. Indeed the stress of a grand prix weekend was often relieved by some practical jokes, usually with Gerhard having a laugh at Ayrton's expense. But the Brazilian learnt to give as good as he got, until this scenario developed a competitive element, sometimes involving Ron himself. On the other hand, the generally relaxed atmosphere did not mean there were no criticisms or doubts to be raised and indeed Senna was troubled by these at the start of this 1991 season.

The Paulista was only half convinced after trying the MP4/6 for the first time. He felt that overall, the chassis was better than its predecessor, but could only find very slight progress as far as Honda's new V12 was concerned. His mood grew sullen after the first few Grands Prix of the season and it was clear to onlookers that he was acting like a spoilt child who was never happy. Not only had he won the first four races, but he had started them ALL from pole and had a considerable lead over his potential rivals, such as Prost, Mansell, Piquet and Berger. *What more did he want?* There was talk of boredom: his triumphant start to the year left him like a king alone and isolated by his implacable dominance. It was not the case.

Senna was totally convinced that his results owed more to a complete lack of real opposition rather than to the qualities of his car. Ferrari was only running an interim car, while Williams was climbing the walls trying to cope with a new and capricious semi-automatic gearbox. Inspired by Ferrari's experiments in 1989, Williams had opted for this system and Senna was furious that McLaren, for reasons of nervousness and tradition had not gone down the same route. It seemed obvious to him that this type of gear change was quicker and was perfectly suited to the modern electronic systems now in use. The problem eventually reared its head at the mid-point of the season. After the German Grand Prix, Ayrton's lead had evaporated like an ice cube on the Equator, as Williams had totally dominated the summer races. Following criticism, the Honda engineers tried to get more power out of the V12, to rival the Renault V10. But they could not find enough horses in Mexico and France and the result was catastrophic in England, and especially in Germany where poor Ayrton ran out of fuel on the last lap, having spent the previous two races with one eye on the fuel gauge. The increase in power from the Japanese engine carried a heavy penalty in terms of fuel consumption. At Silverstone, Senna returned to the pits after running out of fuel, sitting on the side pod of Mansell's winning Williams, putting up with the partisan crowd cheering their moustachioed hero along the way. It was enough to make the hot headed Brazilian's blood boil.

Everything came right at the Hungaroring. Senna soothed his troubled mind with a win and made peace with Prost. On the track, his race consisted of starting ahead of Mansell and Patrese in the Williams, then keeping them under control for 77 laps on a track where it is pretty much impossible to overtake, just as Thierry Boutsen had done the previous year. McLaren came up with a lighter chassis and Honda produced a more powerful qualifying engine. The team even tried a semi-automatic gearbox in practice, but it was not yet race ready. In the

paddock, Ayrton and Alain locked themselves away in the Elf motorhome to discuss their rivalry. At the slightest provocation, these two were at one another's throats and the governing body decided it had had enough of these squabbles. After the sermons, the two men stayed talking together for an hour and a half. They realised that their spat was simply making the newspapers happy and rich and it was not worth the bother. Although they did not become the best of friends, they decided to act in a professional and respectful manner towards one another, much to everyone's relief.

The change of fortunes signalled in Hungary was confirmed in Belgium and Senna felt reassured. The twists and turns of Budapest are hardly a reference point when it comes to race circuits, whereas the track in the Ardennes was unforgiving when it came to a car's set-up. At Spa, the McLaren had greater straight line speed than the Williams, but Ayrton was penalised by an over-long pit stop to change tyres. This let Nigel Mansell through into the lead and Ayrton only won when the Englishman's automatic gearbox played up. That was the key to this contest: the Williams had better performance, but it was less reliable than the McLaren. And Senna had learnt how to look after his car over a race distance. With Mansell showing brilliant if inconsistent form, Ayrton

● **73**_Senna's predictions came true. The summer arrived and Williams' dominance was insolent. At Silverstone he had to endure the misery of Mansell's kindness, as the Brazilian hitched a lift on the sidepod of the victorious Englishman, while the crowd was too happy to care.

• **75_**In 1991, he scored his fourth consecutive win at the marvellous Spa-Francorchamps circuit to equal Jim Clark's acheivement from 1962 to 1965. The Scotsman did it on the old 14.120 km track.

• **74_**Revenge! Finally, Ayrton was able to hold off the Williams on the twisty Hungaroring, where it is impossible to overtake without a willing victim.

learnt to look to the title rather than the wins, something he would never have countenanced two years earlier. In Italy and Portugal, he settled for finishing on the podium and in Spain he really did coast home for points.

It is an interesting exercise to look at the careers of the great drivers and pick out their worst race. Ayrton is no exception to the rule and maybe Barcelona 1991 is his claim to this category. Lying second in the early stages, he tried to hold off Mansell, who was driving like a man possessed. On lap 5, the Englishman popped out from under the McLaren at the entry to the long pit straight and the two cars covered the 1100 metres before the braking area side by side. They rubbed wheels a couple of times and Ayrton had to accept that, on this occasion, Nigel was not going to give up. he braked fractionally early, letting the Englishman through. Then, having regained the lead after the pit stops, Ayrton once again became aware of the Williams whistling along behind him. This time, "the magician" pulled out of his hat nothing more nor less than a simple driving error, spinning his car. Rejoining the race in fourth place, he was easily brushed aside by Alesi in the Ferrari, dropping to fifth. There was little to cheer about in this race, but

the man himself was the first to admit that the two measly points might come in handy at the end of the season. There was no doubt that Ayrton still hated losing as much as ever, but faced with dangerous opposition, he had learnt to salvage what he could.

It was enough for him to head for the penultimate round in Japan as the outright favourite for the world title. With a 16 point lead over Mansell and an equal number of wins, Ayrton could settle for making do with a points finish. He did not. He was determined to make the most of a reinvigorated car thanks to a new fuel recently developed by Shell and he started behind poleman Berger, with Mansell up his exhaust pipes. The Englishman found it hard to keep pace, but tried everything he knew. On lap 10, his Williams, glued to the McLaren diffuser, lost downforce in the fast corner after the pits and ended up in the gravel trap. Ayrton was now world champion for the third time. It fired up its racing spirit and he began to lap even quicker, so that on lap 18, he passed his team-mate, whose engine was losing power. He wanted to win the race to triumph with panache, as he always liked to do. In the end, he let Gerhard re-pass him right at the end of the race, after a painful fight

● **76_**In 1991, as had happened often in the past, the championship was played out in Suzuka. This time the fight was between Senna and Mansell, who only had a slight chance, but threw it away, spinning off behind the Brazilian.

his own conscience, to thank the Austrian who had made several sacrifices for him and had therefore not won a single race that year. Ayrton could thus add to his crown, the title of "knight who rewards his squire". The image was slightly tarnished at the post-race press conference mentioned earlier, when Senna admitted he had forced Prost off the track in 1990.

The new world champion consoled himself for giving away his Japanese win, by taking victory a fortnight later in the streets of Adelaide, which were under water at the time, thanks to a major downpour. The race was stopped after just fourteen laps, as there had been so many crashes in the rain. "The magician" once again demonstrated his mastery of the conditions, splashing serenely through the puddles and could now be considered one of the

most brilliant drivers ever to step into the cockpit of a racing car. With 3 world titles, 33 wins and 60 pole positions, he now took his place alongside such greats as Fangio, Clark, Stewart, Lauda and Prost. He was famous the world over to a sometimes suffocating degree. More so than Prost, he was a prisoner of this celebrity which forced him to sometimes act in a way which the man in the street found hard to understand. He found it more and more difficult to go anywhere without provoking embarrassing bouts of hysteria. Alain Prost had endured a frustrating season and having absented himself from the race tracks in 1992, it left Ayrton Senna as the reference point in Formula 1, without whom the world would stop turning. But his title winning days had in fact ended as the 1991 season came to a close. ■

Eyewitness account of Gerhard Berger

Gerhard was Ayrton's team-mate at McLaren for three years. He pays homage to the man and happily admits to his friend's superiority at the wheel:

"I have to say that honestly, when I came to McLaren, I underestimated Ayrton's performance. I was new in the team and I only had experience of team-mates whom I could beat. I understood very quickly that he was a very special driver. He was not in the same league as anyone I had come across before. What I soon learnt by watching him was that he had no weaknesses, be it as a driver, or in how he set up the car, the way he behaved outside the car and the way he presented himself. He was just the perfect guy! He was a fantastic driver and to beat him on a couple of occasions was a very special pleasure. I think mainly of my first race for McLaren at Phoenix. I was quickest on Friday, it rained on Saturday and so I had pole, while he was only sixth. But I had a crash in the race and Ayrton won. Then he thought about that qualifying session again (I am sure he was really pissed off!) and I never ever beat him again (laughs). No, actually I beat him three times after that. (Author's note. During their time together, Gerhard took four pole positions.) And I set a few fastest race laps, and won three grands prix, but that's all. He had a power of concentration which was above anything I had come across before. When he was concentrating, nothing could interrupt or affect him. He could move mountains when he was in this mood. It was his great strength. He was really the best driver I have ever seen in action. I have always been a realist and I have always tried to be honest with myself. So, from the second season, I realised I would not manage to beat this guy.

We were really good friends and I spent three fantastic years with him at McLaren. We often spoke on the phone, talking about all sorts of things in a very open way, as friends do. For sure, in such an egocentric world you can never be sure of anything, but after his death, I met a lot of people who were very close to him, including his family, who confirmed that our friendship was the real thing."

● **77**_The Grand Prix in the streets of Adelaide seemed more like a powerboat regatta than a car race. Ayrton once again demonstrated his skill in these conditions, although he claimed he did not like them any more than the next man, even though he seemed to adapt better to the wet.

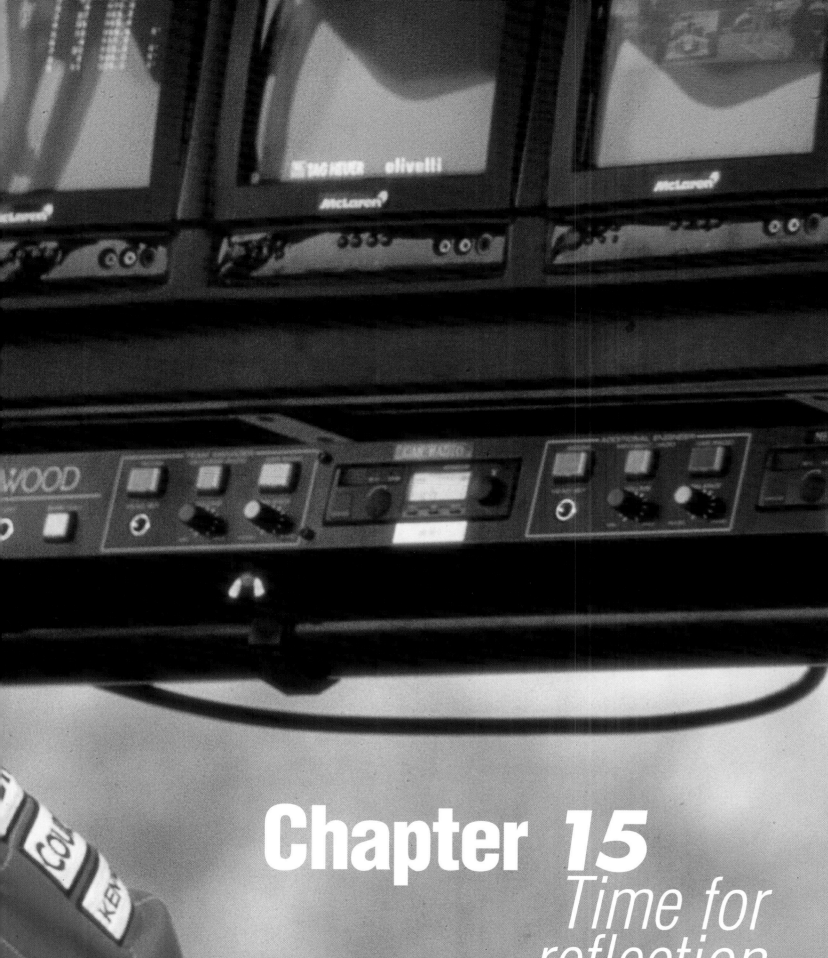

Chapter 15
Time for reflection

• **78_**"*My God, what can I do?*' a dazed Senna seems to be asking himself at the start of the 1992 season, faced with the terrible domination of the active suspension Williams-Renault.

At the end of the 1991 season, McLaren had taken its fourth consecutive Constructors' title and Honda its sixth as engine supplier. However, the last chapter of this record achievement did not come easy. If it had not been for Williams arising late from its slumbers and then having an erratic season, neither Senna nor McLaren would have been able to polish these latest much envied additions to their trophy cabinets. That does not mean they did not deserve their reward, as exploiting your rivals' weaknesses has always been part of the game for the great teams, as well as making up for any deficiencies on your own side of course. Ayrton had already highlighted the team's weak point, namely the manual gearbox on the MP4/6B, which was a definite handicap. The chassis was not the best either and Honda had made little progress. The new MP4/7 was fitted with a brand new V12, with a wider angle than its predecessor. It was mated to a chassis boasting improved

aerodynamics, an automatic gearbox and a fly-by-wire throttle system which was controlled by electronic impulses. The technical project had impressed Senna, but the delay in getting it running less so. That was caused by frantic attempts to improve the MP4/6B at the end of the previous season, so that the new car was not ready for the start of the 1992 season in South Africa, finally rolling out of the transporter for the fourth round in Spain.

The MP4/7 was given its race debut earlier than planned in the Brazilian Grand Prix. For Senna, that was almost too late. Williams had pulled active suspension out of its hat which meant all the other teams would be struggling to catch up. Nigel Mansell was beginning to make a habit of standing on top of the podium. More embarrassing still, the Englishman was beating poor Ayrton to pole position by around two seconds! A whiff of panic hovered over Woking, as the MP4/7 development programme was

Designer: Neil Oatley

Engine

Make/Type: Honda RA 122-EB
Number of Cylinders/Configuration: V12 (Rear)
Capacity: 3493 cc
Bore/Stroke: not given
Compression ratio: not given
Maximum power: 770 hp
Maximum revs: 14500 rpm
Block material: Aluminium
Fuel/Oil: Shell
Sparking plugs: NGK
Injection: Honda
Valve gear: 4 OHC
Number of valves per cylinder: 4
Ignition: Honda
Weight: 140 kg

Transmission

Gearbox/Number of gears: McLaren (6)
Clutch: not given

Chassis

Type: Carbon monocoque
Suspensions: Double wishbones, pushrods (Front and Rear)
Shock absorbers: Showa
Rim diameter: 13" (Front and Rear)
Rim width: 12" (Front) / 16,3" (Rear)
Tyres: Goodyear
Brakes: Brembo discs

Dimensions

Wheelbase: 2972 mm
Track: 1824 mm (Front) / 1679 mm (Rear)
Dry weight: 505 kg
Fuel capacity: 235 litres

Raced from Brazil to Australia.
(MP4/6B raced from South Africa to Mexico – identical tech spec to MP4/6)

hurried along. After the fifth round of the championship in Imola, Mansell took his fifth consecutive win and Senna did not mince his words, saying the season was ruined because the McLaren lacked active suspension, pointing out that the technical team had been slow off the mark in developing the new technology. Ron Dennis dodged the subject, saying the car had "real potential" and the delay actually stemmed from the previous year. Ayrton was not impressed, looking for more than words of comfort and the mood between the two men turned a bit sour.

The Brazilian often looked strained and worried this year, as he was not winning, or hardly ever. Inevitably one returns to his obsession with perfection, with winning all the time. He could not bear to drive, watching powerless as the others accumulated wins. His statements confirmed that as far as he was concerned, finishing second or third or retiring

were all the same to him. It was clear to see he was suffering. He was having to learn to put up with picking up points. The strain showed in his driving. He made uncharacteristic errors at the wheel, running into the back of Brundle in Italy and Mansell in Australia.

In the end, he took three lucky wins in Monaco, Budapest and Monza, making the most of the circumstances on each occasion. In the Principality, he still took great enjoyment from his win, even though it only came to him when Mansell's dominant Williams ran into bother. His fifth victory here meant he equalled Graham Hill's record and was presented with a special trophy to commemorate the achievement. But the odd ray of sunshine could not shift the clouds of a ruined season. There were bigger black clouds heading his way from the land of the rising sun. He was more and more convinced that Honda would pull out of the sport at the end of the season. The news was announced at the Italian Grand Prix.

Despite winning at Monza, Ayrton could not hide his sadness at the fact that those who had powered him on three occasions to racing nirvana were moving on. Dennis was convinced his driver would leave him without a good engine and tried all he knew to get the Renault V10 for 1993. He even considered buying the Ligier team which was using the French engine. To no avail. Renault-Sport President Patrick Faure was inflexible and Ayrton Senna started to look around the paddock. In Hungary, he won only because Mansell decided to settle for a safe second place on his way to the championship title which was his when he stepped onto the

Budapest podium. Ayrton then jokingly announced that he was so impressed with the Williams that he was prepared to drive it for nothing the following year. The off the cuff remark sparked much debate.

For several seasons now, driver salaries were going through the roof and it was beginning to worry the team bosses. Frank Williams, well known for not being over generous towards his drivers, was more than vexed when a newly-crowned Nigel Mansell put in a huge if naïve salary request for 1993. There are no secrets in Formula 1 and this is what prompted Senna's "free offer" after the race in Monza, in the hope

• **79**_Senna took his second win of the season at the Hungaroring, as against Nigel Mansell's eight so far (here behind Ayrton). The game was over and the Brazilian was already thinking about how to improve things for 1993.

• **80**_Seeking advice on his future, Ayrton Senna contacted his old friend Emerson Fittipaldi, who suggested switching to Indycars in the United States. Formula 1 came very close to losing its master.

● **81**_One of the greatest drives in the history of Formula 1. At Donington in 1993, Ayrton Senna lived up to his "magic" nickname. It is still the first lap and the Brazilian has already passed Schumacher and Wendlinger. He then dealt with Hill and Prost to lead the field into lap 2!

of attracting Frank's attention. He hit the target, as Williams immediately opened discussions with the Brazilian, making it clear that Mansell's future did not lie with his team. However, the Brazilian was unaware that Prost had made the most of his "sabbatical" year to prepare his return. Frank Williams accepted the reasonable demands of the Frenchman, as well as a special clause in his contract stipulating that, under no circumstances, would he team up with Ayrton Senna. By the time the Brazilian found out, it was too late and at the Portuguese Grand Prix, Williams announced that Alain Prost would partner Damon Hill in 1993. Acting like a spoilt child denied his favourite toy, Senna accused the Frenchman of being a coward, vowing to go out of his way to beat him on the track the following year. It was a cry of despair given that Ayrton did not even know what he would be driving at that time.

As Ron Dennis had nothing credible to offer him, "the magician" seriously considered leaving Formula 1, rather than having to go through another mediocre year. On the advice of Emerson Fittipaldi, who in the Eighties had become a champion again, this time on the other side of the Atlantic, he went to Phoenix in December to try a Penske Indy car. The test took place at the little Firebird circuit, which was quite a bit slower than a typical Indy track, but it was enough to get an idea of what the car could do. Ayrton enjoyed driving the Penske, finding it quite powerful, despite its extra weight which made it

less lively than a Formula 1 car. The test rekindled his enthusiasm for driving, but he took no decision, preferring to wait and see what Ron Dennis could come up with. As he did every winter, he then went to charge his batteries in his beautiful ocean-side villa at Angra Dos Rei, where he could relax and enjoy his favourite pastimes of jet-skiing, water skiing, tennis and flying model aircraft. He made the most of his free time to launch an initiative which had been dear to his heart for several years. Although he came from a comfortable background, Ayrton had always been aware of the frightening level of poverty which was like a cancer in his beloved home country. He had sworn he would do something about it once he had the means. Now that he was one of the best paid sportsmen on the planet, the time had come. He launched a cartoon strip featuring a little lad called Senninha. The simple aim was to encourage youngsters to live by a set of values which Ayrton had always applied to his own life, in an attempt to help them make the grade. Because of his star status in Brazil, the project was an immediate success. Alongside the cartoon strip, he also set up a foundation, with the help of his sister Viviane, to raise funds by exploiting his name and image. The Instituto Ayrton Senna saw the light of day, but sadly not until a few months after the death of its founder.

During this time, Dennis was doing his utmost to put together a solid technical project around the Ford V8 engine which he had just acquired and which already powered the

• **82**_On the Donington podium, Ayrton Senna, alongside circuit owner Tom Wheatcroft, savours having wiped the floor with his opponents. Damon Hill cannot understand what happened and Alain Prost smiles, precisely because he understands only too well.

● **83**_With a sixth victory in the Principality, Ayrton Senna eclipses the old record, held since 1969 by Damon Hill's father Graham.

Benettons. Flavio Briatore's team had performed more than acceptably with this power plant, thanks mainly to the capabilities of the sport's newest star, Michael Schumacher. Senna did not think much of this as a means of moving forward and negotiations were never ending. The 1993 season was about to start and Ron was on the verge of having a heart attack. He still did not have a number one driver to pair up with Gerhard Berger's replacement, Michael Andretti. Hedging his bets and as a failsafe move, he hired the promising young Finn, Mika Hakkinen. But the youngster would have to step down to the role of test driver, if the Brazilian star finally agreed to come back to work.

This Ayrton finally did, albeit grudgingly, but on one condition: he only signed up for the first race in South Africa. There, he would make a decision as to whether the equipment at his disposal made it worth his while continuing. He only arrived in England a few days before the season curtain-raiser, gave his MP4/8-Ford a

quick test at Silverstone and flew off to Kyalami. After the South African Grand Prix, Senna had learnt two facts: his new car had a "surprising" potential, but it was still the case that he had been powerless to do anything to beat Alain Prost in the Williams-Renault. The Frenchman was immediately made outright favourite to take the title and maybe it was this irritating prospect which pushed an unconvinced Senna to try and put a spoke in his rival's wheels. After the European Grand Prix he was delighted and had no regrets.

The fun started at home in Interlagos. The Williams were dominant, but the character of the race changed completely and in apocalyptic fashion with a terrible tropical storm which burst at half-distance. Prost slid off the track, as did several others and the pace car was called out while the wreckage was removed. Once the race was underway again, Senna made the most of the damp track to attack and devour the inexperienced Hill, who was out of his depth. The samba bands were on full song again and so was the challenge. A fortnight later, the Donington circuit in England hosted its first Formula 1 race in modern times, in typically English cold and rain. The conditions changed throughout the race, giving drivers and teams a very big strategic headache. Ayrton was only fifth at the first corner after the start, but on the cold and greasy track, he charged through to the front in just one lap. It was a display of total supremacy. While Prost and Hill made seven pit stops to change to and from rain tyres, Senna only came in five times. It was a breathtaking display which put every other man on the track to shame. The race is quite rightly considered as one of his best ever drives, reminiscent of a performance by that other "magician" Stirling Moss, when the Englishman and his Lotus-Climax embarrassed the far more powerful Ferrari's at Monaco in 1961.

In the post-race press conference, Prost, complete with a long face, explained that his much envied Williams had not worked well that day. Senna turned to him and smiled, before offering to swap cars!

Two grands prix later and against all odds, Ayrton Senna was leading the championship, thanks to another win in the streets of Monaco no less! He was now the outright record holder for the event, but he remained level headed. He owed his win to an unjust penalty imposed on

● **84**_"My mate Prost" and "my mate Senna" on the podium in Australia, together for the last time. In 1994, Alain Prost had retired and Ayrton would never stand on a podium again…

● **85**_After a season spent in the Williams' shadow, Ayrton was back to his winning ways in Japan, on a track which had seen so many of the key moments in his career, in front of a crowd which idolised him.

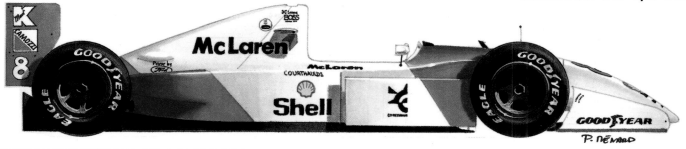

Designer: Neil Oatley

Engine

Make/Type: Ford Cosworth HB
Number of Cylinders/Configuration: V8 (Rear)
Capacity: 3494 cc
Bore/Stroke: not given
Compression ratio: not given
Maximum power: 700 hp
Maximum revs: 13200 rpm
Block material: Aluminium
Fuel/Oil: Shell
Sparking plugs: NGK
Injection: not given
Valve gear: 4 OHC
Number of valves per cylinder: 4
Ignition: not given
Weight: 135 kg

Transmission

Gearbox/Number of gears: McLaren (6)
Clutch: not given

Chassis

Type: Carbon monocoque
Suspensions: Wishbones, pushrods (Front and Rear)
Shock absorbers: Showa
Rim diameter: 13" (Front and Rear)
Rim width: 11,5" (Front) / 13,8" (Rear)
Tyres: Goodyear
Brakes: Brembo discs

Dimensions

Wheelbase: 2902 mm
Track: 1626 mm (Front) / 1607 mm (Rear)
Dry weight: 505 kg
Fuel capacity: 215 litres

Used all season.

Alain Prost, who left the pits in 22nd position. He knew that this minor fairy tale was about to come to an end. The summer calendar featured circuits where the Renault V10 would be able to stretch its legs, showing up the weaknesses of his humble V8. That indeed is what happened and the Brazilian would not be seen on the top step of the podium until the final two races of the season at Suzuka and Adelaide. In both cases, he drove a perfect race and the Williams team lacked some motivation, given that a fortnight earlier they had picked up both the Constructors' and the Drivers' titles courtesy of Prost. Nevertheless, Ayrton had a good season with five wins, all down to his undeniable talent for getting the best out of a car which really was nothing much to write home about. He increased his record for pole positions to a fantastic 62 and with 41 wins to his name, he planned to make inroads on Alain Prost's record which had now stopped at 51. Because in 1994, Senna would be with Williams and Prost had retired.

Having secured a fourth title, the Frenchman had decided to hang up his helmet. Tired of all the politics and intrigue in the F1 circus, he knew that Frank Williams was very keen to have Ayrton in his team. He therefore preferred to give up his seat. The news was a bombshell, as many expected Prost to go after the record of five titles which had been held by the peerless Juan Manuel Fangio for thirty six years. As soon as the rumour hit the Estoril paddock, Ayrton headed for the one man who could fill him on what was happening. French journalist Lionel Froissart knew both men well and Senna trusted him implicitly. The Frenchman confirmed the news and Ayrton seemed shell-shocked: his reference point, his alter ego was leaving him. Who would he measure up to in the future? ∎

Chapter 16
"I miss you Alain"

The handshake was firm and sincere, peppered with the flashguns fired by the photographers. The two men, the smaller of the two in blue, the other in red, looked one another in the eye. The emotion was visible as Ayrton Senna and Alain Prost stood on the Adelaide podium. Alain had just finished the last race of his fabulous motor racing career. Ayrton had just won his last race for McLaren, the team he was leaving with a heavy heart. The Woking team had brought him everything in terms of money and glory. He had forged an indestructible bond of friendship with Ron Dennis, but he simply could not accept Ron's long term plan which involved developing the new McLaren-Peugeot. It would take too long and Ayrton wanted to be world champion again as soon as possible and Williams was his best option.

Ayrton and Alain spoke to the journalists during the press conference. They were relaxed and even jocular as they discussed the past. For Senna, the duel had come to an end, with no winners or losers. He was convinced he would beat the Frenchman's records, but he knew he would feel a certain nostalgia, a "saudade" as they say in Brazil, when he would lead the field next year without his rival at his side. In the end

he had always respected- well almost always- and admired his opponent and the feeling was mutual. He would simply have to get used to doing without him and find his motivation from the new challenge he had set himself.

At the start of 1994, Ayrton Senna was wearing new colours; those of team sponsor Rothmans. However, he still kept the famous Nacional logo on his race suit. The Brazilian bank had been a constant personal sponsor since 1985 and he had already insisted on it at McLaren. Damon Hill was to be his team-mate. Graham's son had made enormous progress thanks to working with Prost and was counting on making the most of having a new and highly talented teacher to improve his technical understanding still further. Frank Williams was happy. After Piquet, Mansell and Prost, he was about to employ the final member of the quartet which had dominated Formula 1 for over a decade.

As always in the winter, the teams tested endlessly to develop their new cars. One of these sessions took place in 1994 at the Imola circuit in Italy. With the backing of other drivers, Ayrton complained to the circuit management about destabilising bumps in the high speed Tamburello corner. The San Marino Grand Prix was due to

Eyewitness account of Jacques Laffite

Jean-François Galeron

The popular French driver recalls two stories from different moments in the Senna era:

"Like Lauda, Prost and Schumacher today, Senna was a hard worker. All the great champions are. But he also had the talent, because without talent one achieves nothing. He could seem a bit cold, but he tried to get on with everyone. He was kind and polite.

I remember in Brazil, the first time he raced in Formula 1, I was in a restaurant with some friends and we saw him. We knew he was good, but as a new driver, we did not think about it much: we had seen so many! But he sent us over a bottle of wine, saying "Welcome to Brazil." I thought this was a nice gesture. For a young driver to make his mark on the track is one thing, but this gesture touched me.

The last time I met him was in 1994 during a friendly France-Brazil football match. He was there to kick off the game, on the Saturday before the race week at Imola. We spoke for a long time about racing and his car. He was asking himself a lot of questions about the safety of his car and the difficulty he had in setting it up. He did not think it was very good, but he was confident, knowing that he had to work to sort it out. But he was on pole at Imola don't forget! As to the causes of his death, there is not much left to say. Something broke and there you have it. We will never know and then again, we don't care. He died stupidly, like a lot of others before him unfortunately. But he was a nice lad."

● **87**_For the second time in two races, Ayrton Senna's race ended prematurely. In Brazil, it was his own fault, but here at Ti-Aida, it was the unfortunate Nicola Larini who speared the Williams' side pod with his Ferrari.

take place there in less than two months. The organisers agreed to get rid of the worst of the bumps, as a more complete solution would be too time consuming.

The season curtain raiser took place at Interlagos. Much to the delight of the huge partisan crowd in the grandstands, the local hero in his new blue and white livery took pole position, three tenths of a second ahead of Michael Schumacher in the Benetton. Despite this encouraging performance, Ayrton seemed more worried than usual. He explained that his car was very twitchy and difficult to control and that he felt cramped in the cockpit. In the race, he went off the track trying to catch the leader Schumacher. He admitted it was his mistake, after being caught out by the brutal power delivery of the Renault V10 and the lack of traction control, which was now banned. Three weeks later, he was again on pole at the Aida circuit, which staged the new Pacific Grand Prix. To those who reckoned the Williams was the best car on the grid, Ayrton pointed out that a qualifying lap was very different to a race and he was not sure he could maintain that sort of pace over 83 laps, at the wheel of such a difficult beast. He never found out if he could as, shortly after the start, he was hit from behind by Nicola

Larini in the Ferrari, who was trying to avoid Hakkinen's McLaren. He was reduced to the role of spectator, with plenty of time to assess the situation. Schumacher had picked up an easy second win and already had a 20 point lead over Senna, whose confidence level was low. He was worried that the FW16 might spoil the dreams he had when thinking of the Renault engine at the end of the previous year. Would the Williams team give him the wherewithal to show off his talents as he had done at McLaren? After Piquet, Mansell and Prost, was he just another "driving machine" for the inflexible Frank? Strangely, he appeared less self-confident, more withdrawn. He seemed to have difficulty communicating with his engineers and his incredible determination appeared to have dropped a notch, as though the whole business was less important to him than before.

Saturday 30th April 1994: Ayrton Senna's Williams was out on the Imola track for free practice. The Brazilian champion was supposed to be giving a live commentary for French television, a job imposed on him by his French engine supplier. As he rolled down the main pit straight, he uttered the immortal line: *"First of all, I would like to say, Alain, I miss you!"* A joke to break the ice or a heartfelt sentiment? It was

● **88**_Imola, San Marino Grand Prix, 1st May 1994: The Safety Car sets the pace for the pack, led by Senna, Schumacher and Berger, while debris is swept away after the collision between Lehto and Lamy. In a few laps, the race would be on again, but just for a couple of laps.

Designer: Adrian Newey

Engine

Make/Type: Renault RS6
Number of Cylinders/Configuration: V10 (Rear)
Capacity: 3493 cc
Bore/Stroke: not given
Compression ratio: not given
Maximum power: 790 hp
Maximum revs: 14800 rpm
Block material: Aluminium
Fuel/Oil: Elf
Sparking plugs: Champion
Injection: not given
Valve gear: 4 OHC
Number of valves per cylinder: 4
Ignition: Magneti Marelli
Weight: 134 kg

Transmission

Gearbox/Number of gears: Williams (6)
Clutch: not given

Chassis

Type: Carbon monocoque
Shock absorbers: Showa
Rim diameter: 13 " (Front and Rear)
Rim width: 11,5 " (Front) / 13" (Rear)
Tyres: Goodyear
Brakes: AP Racing discs

Dimensions

Wheelbase: 2990 mm
Track: 1670 mm (Front) / 1600 mm (Rear)
Dry weight: 505 kg
Fuel capacity: 210 litres

Raced from Brazil to San Marino.

probably a bit of both. This season certainly had an unfamiliar feeling to it for the superstar who no longer had a mirror to reflect his talent. He was alone in a pack of young lions whom he did not know very well; Hill, Schumacher and Hakkinen. Of the old brigade, there was only his mate Gerhard Berger, Jean Alesi and his old F3 adversary Martin Brundle, who had replaced him at McLaren. But he was not fighting with the old guard and that is what he found strange.

Then there was the question of safety. The man who many regarded as something of a hothead seemed more and more concerned with this issue. Senna had been deeply upset by his fellow countryman Rubens Barrichello's spectacular accident in the Jordan the day before. Fortunately, Barrichello emerged relatively unscathed. That was not to be the case the next day. At 14h18 on Saturday, Rookie Roland Ratzenberger's Simtek lost part of its front wing

at over 300 km/h on the long straight following Tamburello. It then swerved off the track and hit the wall on the outside of Villeneuve corner. It was a terrifyingly heavy impact. The unfortunate Austrian was extracted from the wreckage in a coma and died shortly afterwards. Profoundly shocked, Ayrton requisitioned a Safety Car and went to the scene of the accident to try and understand what had happened. In fact, he was later reprimanded by officials for doing so. As a sign of respect, he, along with Damon Hill and the Benetton drivers, did not continue with the session when it was restarted.

That night, he called his girlfriend, Adriana Galisteu, in Portugal to tell her he would probably not take part in the race. In the end, he changed his mind the following morning having resolved to get far more involved in safety at the grands prix, using his experience to guide those working on this matter.

Eyewitness account of Alain Prost

In 1994, Alain Prost and Ayrton Senna were back on speaking terms, but sadly it was not to last long. The French champion recalled there unusual relationship:

"He called me a lot and was nice on the phone. I have to say it was amazing for me to hear this. To a certain extent, I had found the man again. He even tried to persuade me to drive the McLaren with the Peugeot engine! Because he did not feel motivated about fighting against Schumacher and all the youngsters. Then, he asked me a lot of questions about the car and I think he was a little bit disappointed with the handling of the Williams, especially in terms of the physical difficulty of driving it. I confirmed that I had also had a lot of trouble in finding a comfortable driving position as the steering wheel was mounted very low... Then there was the matter of the team. He was surprised by the atmosphere. He had always known life at McLaren where everything went smoothly for him, even in our last season together. It's possible to have a problem with one or two people, but with the rest of the team, the atmosphere was extraordinary. But at Williams, it was very tough. I think he had expected something different.

At Imola, I saw him throughout the weekend. He was already in turmoil. He had called me the week before and asked me," Would you like to be president of the GPDA, because we have to do something about safety." You have to understand that recently, even before moving to Williams, he had softened his approach and he had developed a sense of responsibility. Then, during the weekend, I was at Renault, whom I was working for as well as doing commentary and each time he came out of the Williams motorhome, he came to see me. I was very surprised. I remember having lunch before the race with around half a dozen VIPs. He swung by our motorhome, in amongst all these people, which was unbelievable because when you are concentrating, you go straight to your garage. He wanted to tell me something yet again, although today, I can't remember what it was. It really surprised me! Twenty minutes before the start, I went into the Williams garage. He was behind the banks of computers, all alone looking at the data. I went to wish him good luck for the race, nothing more. And at that point and there is no other word for it, he looked very upset. He was not well. Mind you, he could often be like that before a race. At McLaren, I can remember him locking himself in the toilet for twenty minutes and we wondered what he was doing. But on this occasion it was different. It is the last image I have of him. Not on the grid, but in the garage, all alone with his thoughts."

The next day, all eyes were focussed on the Brazilian as usual; maybe a bit more than usual. All the photos tell a story: the drawn face of a man going through internal turmoil and anxiety, finding it hard to concentrate. But at 2 pm, all that was swept aside as the professional driver took control again for the start, determined to make the most of his 65th pole set on Friday. He was leading the opening lap with Schumacher and Berger tailing him, when the red flag was waved and the Safety Car came out to lead them round. Ayrton was driving carefully, coming through the Variante Bassa and onto the pit straight. He saw debris on the track and the marshals busy working. On the team radio, he learnt that JJ Lehto's Benetton had stalled on the grid and had been hit from behind by Pedro Lamy's Lotus. Apparently there were no injuries, although later it transpired that several members of the public had been hurt by flying debris. What was going through his mind? For six laps behind the Safety Car, Ayrton must certainly have been struggling to maintain his motivation, while trying to find out more about what was going on as each lap ticked by. At the same time,

he was zig-zagging his car to keep temperature in the tyres, while checking engine temperatures and pressures. The race was about to start again and on lap 5, the lights went green indicating that the race would be on again next time round. Ayrton accelerated again before the Variante Bassa and ripped across the line with the same pursuers on his heels. It was lap 6.

He came into Tamburello at about 300 km/h and his car smashed heavily into the track at the exact point where it had been resurfaced, as per his request back in March. There were a few patches of darker asphalt showing where the work had been done. Schumacher was right on his tail and Senna knew the young German would be hard to shake off. When he came past the pits again, the Benetton was a few car lengths behind the Williams. Even though they were already racing hard, the drivers were still wary of the track surface, looking out for any debris left over from the crash at the start. Senna went up through the gears and the Williams roared down the pit straight. Lap 7. The next short straight was swallowed up in a handful of seconds and the long fast Tamburello corner loomed again. The corner could be taken flat out without any bother, as long as the driver stayed exactly on the racing line, which is pretty much the case for any flat out corner on any circuit in the world.

Ayrton turned the wheel to the left and began to fight the force which naturally pushed his helmet to the outside. The car jumped over the strips of asphalt. He applied a tiny bit of opposite lock, as if preparing to correct any oversteer. Suddenly, the Williams jumped out of line and the steering wheel moved from side to side in an abnormal fashion. Something had gone very wrong. The car began to oversteer and then the nose headed for the outside of the corner, towards the concrete wall close to the outside of the track. It could not be placed any further back, as there was a stream running behind it. The foot came off the throttle pedal. Everything was happening very very quickly. Just two seconds. The driver tried to brake, pressing harder and harder on the middle pedal. The car jumped over the grass verge and landed on the tarmac. The foot went back on the throttle as the driver tried to get the rear wheels to grip again. Although the car had slowed considerably, it was still travelling at over 220 km/h. A few metres from the wall, what did Ayrton see in his mind? Did he remember his first drive at Interlagos, in the crepuscular light of a tropical storm? Did he see the thousands of hands applauding him from below as he stood on the podium. Who and what did he see? Not the black and broken piece of suspension which pierced his helmet. ■

"Nada pode me separar do amor de Deus" (*)

(*): Nothing can separate me from the love of God

• **89**_The exit to Tamburello and its famous wall. Definitely too close to the track.

Chapter 17
The memory

The shock waves caused by the death of Ayrton Senna that Sunday 1st May 1994 were as terrible and powerful as the strength of the concrete wall at Tamburello. Twenty six years earlier, that other seemingly invincible tightrope walker, Jim Clark, died in similar circumstance, creating a sad void for racing enthusiasts. Like Ayrton, he was pretty much the favourite to walk off with the title at the start of that season, which he was due to tackle in the superb Lotus 49. That's where the comparison ends as times and customs were very different back then.

Hardly anyone witnessed the death of Jim Clark, in an unimportant Formula 2 race which was of little interest to anyone, least of all Clark himself. Ayrton Senna died in people's living rooms through the medium of live television during a Formula 1 world championship race which drew huge media coverage. Sadly, Senna's death followed the rules of media and marketing, with viewers the world over watching lengthy images of a human being dying. This is the

unfortunate law of the cathode ray tube which cannot differentiate between the death throes of a world renowned sportsman and some anonymous natural disaster. Senna and Ratzenberger died on consecutive days; one was very well known, the other was making his debut out of the limelight. The Italian legal system set up a lengthy inquest to try and find the cause of the Brazilian's death, looking for culprits to blame, but nothing similar was applied to the poor Austrian and his Simtek. Two deaths, two different measures.

The motor racing world was left totally incredulous. The general feeling was that all the various safety measures put into place over the past few years had borne fruit and no one could conceive of such a tragedy. Furthermore, the "magician" who triumphed over the elements had been regarded as invincible. In people's subconscious, he had taken on the aura of a mystical and immortal being. In this respect, Senna was different to all the other drivers. His religious beliefs, his capacity for concentration and isolation, his driving; everything set him resolutely apart. His death became the last stone in the temple of his deification. Naturally, in Brazil, the pain of his death was felt deeply. An entire nation grieved for its hero, who in the same way as Pele and Fittipaldi had raised the country's profile on foreign shores. As a special mark of respect, three days of national mourning were announced and the Paulista was buried with full state honours. Apart from Piquet, for obvious reasons and Gugelmin, who was too upset to attend, every well known Brazilian racing driver accompanied their friend, their brother to his final resting place in the verdant and tranquil Morumbi cemetery. Alain Prost also helped bear the weight of the coffin, while Ron Dennis and Frank Williams were in the crowd.

As expected, the Italian judiciary instigated an investigation to find out why the Williams had suddenly left the track at Tamburello corner on lap 7 of the San Marino Grand Prix. The car was impounded in a run down hangar where it was left to rot away for three years, as the enquiry rumbled on. Detailed study of the telemetry data revealed that "*something sudden and abnormal had taken place on the car and that driver error could be ruled out.*" Three hypotheses were then put forward to explain the "destabilising element". They were, bumps in the corner, a broken steering column under full load, debris on the track leading to a puncture. Watching the film (available on the internet) one can indeed see the Williams jump as it goes over those bands of new tarmac. Telemetry indicates that Senna is forced to make corrections to his line with a sudden turn on the wheel. But, as a driver pointed out, all the cars went through this process at Tamburello and the corner was only dangerous if there was already a problem with the car. The problem with the steering column was subject to much more controversy and in 1997 the Italian procurator overseeing the hearing, charged Frank Williams, Patrick Head and Adrian Newey with culpable homicide. The column was found to be broken, but was this the cause or a result of the impact with the wall?

● **91**_The Williams wreck is removed from the circuit. It is evident that the survival cell has stood up perfectly well to the impact, but the right front suspension is missing.

● **92**_At the 1995 San Marino Grand Prix, hundreds of floral tributes of affection were laid at the scene of the previous year's accident.

The column had been modified, at Senna's request, to make his legs more comfortable in the cockpit. A thinner piece of tubing had been welded onto the original part and it was this additional part which had broken. It was impossible to prove that the sudden movements of the steering wheel were caused by a broken column and neither was there any proof that metal fatigue had caused the failure. The only fact was that the work had been carried out correctly. Charges against the Williams hierarchy were dropped. As for the puncture theory, photographs were produced shortly before the Italian tribunal, showing debris on the track on the line taken by the Williams. Once the car went over it, the debris had moved. The state of the wrecked car and its wheels made it impossible to verify this theory, but it seems an unlikely cause of the Williams's sudden change of attitude.

The matter was therefore closed and the most likely hypothesis was the broken steering column, although it could not be proved. What is certain is that, in hitting the wall on the right side at a fairly shallow angle of 22 degrees, the cockpit stood up well to the impact. It was a piece of suspension which pierced Senna's helmet at the speed of a bullet. When the safety crew arrived on the scene, they must have realised immediately that the situation was hopeless. Once stabilised and still showing signs of life, Ayrton was flown by helicopter to the Maggiore hospital in Bologna where attempts were made to resuscitate him. Gerhard Berger was one of the first to arrive after the race and saw that his friend was being kept alive artificially. At 18h45, the news of Ayrton Senna's death was officially communicated to the world. ■

STATISTICS

Titles won

_KARTING

1976	Brazilian Champion, Junior category
1977	South American Champion, Inter category
1978	Brazilian Champion, Inter category
1979	Runner-up, World Inter category
1980	Brazilian Champion, Inter category
	South American Champion, Inter category
	Runner-up, World Inter category

_SINGLE SEATERS

1981	English Formula Ford 1600 Champion
1982	English Formula Ford 2000 Champion
	European Formula Ford 2000 Champion
1983	English Formula 3 Champion
1988	Formula 1 World Champion
1990	Formula 1 World Champion
1991	Formula 1 World Champion

161 Grands Prix
3 Formula 1 world titles
41 wins, 65 pole positions,
19 fastest race laps

1984

Toleman TG183B- Hart 415T 4L/t from Brazil to San Marino
Toleman TG184- Hart 415T 4L/t from France to Portugal
Tyres Pirelli from Brazil to San Marino, Michelin from France to Portugal

GRAND PRIX		CIRCUIT	QUALIFYING	RACE	RACE TIME
Brazil	25 March	Rio-Jacarepaguà	16th (1:33.525)	Rtd (turbo)	19th (1:42.286)
South Africa	7 April	Kyalami	13th (1:06.981)	6th at 3 laps	15th (1:12.124)
Belgium	29 April	Zolder	19th (1:18.876)	6th at 2 laps (*)	15th (1:22.633)
San Marino	6 May	Imola	Not Qualified	-	-
France	20 May	Dijon-Prenois	13th (1:05.744)	Rtd (turbo)	15th (1:10.100)
Monaco	3 June	Monaco	13th (1:25.009)	2nd at 7.446	FRL* (1:54.334)
Canada	17 June	Montréal-Notre Dame	9th (1:27.448)	7th at 2 laps	3th (1:31.882)
United States	24 June	Detroit	7th (1:42.651)	Rtd (accident)	10th (1:47.444)
Dallas	8 July	Dallas	6th (1:38.256)	Rtd (transmission)	9th (1:46.419)
Great Britain	27 July	Brands Hatch	7th (1:11.890)	3rd at 1:03.328	Rtd (engine)
Germany	5 August	Hockenheim	9th (1:49.395)	Rtd (accident)	11th (1:55.712)
Austria	19 August	Österreichring	10th (1:29.200)	Rtd (oil pressure)	7th (1:34.348)
Netherlands	26 August	Zandvoort	13th (1:15.960)	Rtd (engine)	13th (1:21.683)
Italy	9 September	Monza	Not-entered	-	-
Europe	7 October	Nürburgring	12th (1:22.439)	Rtd (start accident)	-
Portugal	21 October	Estoril	3rd (1:21.936)	3rd at 20:042.	7th (1:24.373)

Position in world championship: 9th ex æquo / 13 points
Average points per race for season: 0.81

*FRL: Fastest Race Lap

(*) Belgium: Senna initially 7th, reclassified after Tyrrells disqualified at end of year

1985

Lotus 97T-Renault EF4 V6/t from Brazil to San Marino
Lotus 97T-Renault EF4/EF15 V6/t from Monaco to Australia

Tyres Goodyear

Brazil	7 April	Rio-Jacarepaguà	4th (1:28.389)	Rtd (electrical)	5th (1:38.440)
Portugal	21 April	Estoril	Pole (1:21.936)	1st 2:00:28.006	FRL (1:44.121)
San Marino	5 May	Imola	Pole (1:27.327)	7th (ran out of fuel)	5th (1:31.549)
Monaco	19 May	Monaco	Pole (1:20.450)	Rtd (engine)	8th (1:24.803)
Canada	16 June	Montréal-Notre Dame	2nd (1:24.816)	16th (turbo)	FRL (1:27.445)
United States	23 June	Detroit	Pole (1:42.051)	Rtd (accident)	FRL (1:45.612)
France	7 July	Paul-Ricard	2nd (1:32.835)	Rtd (engine)	3rd (1:41.552)
Great Britain	21 July	Silverstone	4th (1:06.324)	10th (injection problem)	2nd (1:10.032)
Germany	4 August	Hockenheim	5th (1:18.792)	Rtd (joint failure)	7th (1:24.270)
Austria	18 August	Österreichring	14th (1:28.023)	2nd at 30.002	8th (1:31.666)
Netherlands	25 August	Zandvoort	4th (1:11.837)	3rd at 48.491	7th (1:17.835)
Italy	8 September	Monza	Pole (1:25.084)	3rd at 1:00.390	9th (1:31.703)
Belgium	15 September	Spa-Francorchamps	2nd (1:55.403)	1st 1:34:19.893	5th (2:03.479)
Europe	6 October	Brands Hatch	Pole (1:07.482)	2nd at 21.396	5th (1:12.601)
South Africa	19 October	Kyalami	4th (1:02.825)	Rtd (engine)	7th (1:10.077)
Australia	3 November	Adelaïde	Pole (1:19.843)	Rtd (engine)	2nd (1:24.140)

Position in world championship:
4th/38 points
Laps in lead: 270

7 pole positions, 2 wins, 3 fastest race laps
Kilometres in lead: 1325

Average points per race for season: 2.375

1986 _Lotus 98T-Renault EF15 and 15DP V6/t

Tyres Goodyear

Brazil	23 March	Rio-Jacarepaguà	Pole (1:25.501)	2nd at 34.827	3rd (1:34.785)
Spain	13 April	Jerez	Pole (1:21.605)	1st 1:48:47.735	7th (1:28.801)
San Marino	27 April	Imola	Pole (1:25.050)	Rtd (wheel bearing)	9th (1:31.999)
Monaco	19 May	Monaco	3rd (1:23.175)	3rd at 53.646	2nd (1:26.843)
Belgium	25 May	Spa-Francorchamps	4th (1:54.576)	2nd at 19.827	2nd (1:59.867)
Canada	15 June	Montréal-Notre Dame	2nd (1:24.188)	5th at 1 lap	5th (1:27.479)
United States	22 June	Detroit	Pole (1:38.301)	1st 1:51:12.847	3rd (1:41.552)
France	6 July	Paul-Ricard	Pole (1:06.526)	Rtd (accident)	13th (1:12.882)
Great Britain	13 July	Brands Hatch	3rd (1:07.524)	Rtd (gearbox)	14th (1:14.024)
Germany	27 July	Hockenheim	3rd (1:42.329)	2nd at 15.437	4th (1:49.424)
Hungary	10 August	Hungaroring	Pole (1:29.450)	2nd at 17.673	2nd (1:31.261)
Austria	17 August	Österreichring	8th (1:25.249)	Rtd (engine)	9th (1:33.437)
Italy	7 September	Monza	5th (1:24.916)	Rtd (transmission at start)	-
Portugal	21 September	Estoril	Pole (1:16.673)	4th at 1 lap	4th (1:21.283)
Mexico	12 October	Mexico	Pole (1:16.990)	3rd at 52.513	4th (1:20.237)
Australia	26 October	Adelaïde	3rd (1:18.906)	Rtd (engine)	13th (1:24.149)

Position in world championship:
4th / 55 points
Laps in lead: 135

8 pole positions, 2 wins
Kilometres in lead: 571

Average points per race for season: 3.438

1987 _Lotus 99T-Honda RA168E V6/t in Brazil
Lotus 99T-Honda RA167G V6/t from San Marino to Australia

Tyres Goodyear

Brazil	12 April	Rio-Jacarepaguà	3rd (1:28.408)	Rtd (engine)	5th (1:35.312)
San Marino	3 May	Imola	Pole (1:25.806)	2nd at 27.545	4th (1:30.851)
Belgium	17 May	Spa-Francorchamps	3rd (1:52.426)	Rtd (acc. with Mansell)	-
Monaco	31 May	Monaco	2nd (1:23.711)	1st 1:57:54.085	FRL (1:27.685)
United States	21 June	Detroit	2nd (1:40.607)	1st 1:50:16.358	FRL (1:40.464)
France	5 July	Paul-Ricard	3rd (1:07.024)	4th at 55.255	7th (1:12.231)
Great Britain	12 July	Silverstone	3rd (1:08.181)	3rd at 1 tour	3rd (1:11.605)
Germany	26 July	Hockenheim	2nd (1:42.616)	3rd at 1 tour	4th (1:49.187)
Hungary	9 August	Hungaroring	6th (1:30.387)	2nd at 37.727	4th (1:32.426)
Austria	16 August	Österreichring	7th (1:25.492)	5th at 2 laps	3rd (1:28.449)
Italy	6 September	Monza	4th (1:24.907)	2nd at 1.806	FRL (1:26.796)
Portugal	20 September	Estoril	5th (1:18.354)	7th at 2 laps	3rd (1:20.217)
Spain	27 September	Jerez	5th (1:24.320)	5th at 1:13.507	11th (1:30.088)
Mexico	18 October	Mexico	7th (1:19.089)	Rtd (spin)	3rd (1:20.586)
Japon	1st November	Suzuka	7th (1:42.723)	2nd at 17.384	3rd (1:45.805)
Australia	15 November	Adelaïde	4th (1:18.488)	(2nd, Disqualified)	2nd (1:20.456)

Position in world championship:
3rd / 57 points
Laps in lead: 108

1 pole position, 2 wins, 3 fastest race laps
Kilometres in lead: 278

Average points per race for season: 3.563

1988 _ McLaren MP4/4-Honda RA 168E V6/t

Tyres Goodyear

Brazil	3 April	Rio-Jacarepaguà	**Pole (1:28.096)**	Disqualified	9th (1:34.657)
San Marino	1st May	Imola	**Pole (1:27.148)**	**1st 1:32:41.264**	2nd (1:29.815)
Monaco	15 May	Monaco	**Pole (1:23.998)**	Rtd (accident)	**FRL (1:26.321)**
Mexico	29 May	Mexico	**Pole (1:17.468)**	2nd at 7.104	2nd (1:18.776)
Canada	12 June	Montréal-Notre Dame	**Pole (1:21.681)**	**1st 1:39:46.618**	**FRL (1:24.973)**
United States	19 June	Detroit	**Pole (1:40.606)**	**1st 1:54:56.635**	2nd (1:44.992)
France	3 July	Paul-Ricard	2nd (1:08.067)	2nd at 31.752	2nd (1:11.856)
Great Britain	10 July	Silverstone	3rd (1:10.616)	**1st 1:33:16.376**	4th (1:23.595)
Germany	24 July	Hockenheim	**Pole (1:44.596)**	**1st 1:32:54.188**	3rd (2:05.001)
Hungary	7 August	Hungaroring	**Pole (1:27.635)**	**1st 1:57:47.081**	2nd (1:30.964)
Belgium	28 August	Spa-Francorchamps	**Pole (1:53.718)**	**1st 1:28:00.549**	2nd (2:01.061)
Italy	11 September	Monza	**Pole (1:25.974)**	Rtd (acc. with Schlesser)	3rd (1:29.569)
Portugal	25 September	Estoril	2nd (1:17.869)	6th at 1:18.269	8th (1:22.852)
Spain	2 October	Jerez	**Pole (1:24.067)**	4th at 47.710	3rd (1:28.273)
Japon	1st November	Suzuka	**Pole (1:41.853)**	**1st 1:33:26.176**	**FRL (1:46.326)**
Australia	15 November	Adelaïde	**Pole (1:17.748)**	2nd at 36.787	4th (1:21.668)

Position in world championship:
World Champion / 90 points
Laps in lead: 552

13 pole positions, 8 wins, 3 fastest race laps
Kilometres in lead: 2671

Average points per race for season: 5.875

1989 _ McLaren MP4/5-Honda RA 109E V10

Tyres Goodyear

Brazil	26 March	Rio-Jacarepaguà	**Pole (1:25.302)**	11th at 2 laps	9th (1:33.685)
San Marino	23 April	Imola	**Pole (1:26.010)**	**1st 1:26:51.245**	2nd (1:27.273)
Monaco	7 May	Monaco	**Pole (1:22.308)**	**1st 1:53:33.251**	2nd (1:26.017)
Mexico	28 May	Mexico	**Pole (1:17.876)**	**1st 1:35:21:431**	2nd (1:20.585)
United States	4 June	Phoenix	**Pole (1:30.108)**	Rtd (electrical)	**FRL (1:33.969)**
Canada	18 June	Montréal-Notre Dame	2nd (1:21.049)	Rtd (engine) classified 7th	2nd (1:32.143)
France	9 July	Paul-Ricard	2nd (1:07.228)	Rtd (differential)	-
Great Britain	16 July	Silverstone	**Pole (1:09.099)**	Rtd (spin/gearbox)	4th (1:13.737)
Germany	30 July	Hockenheim	**Pole (1:42.300)**	**1st 1:21:43.302**	**FRL (1:45.884)**
Hungary	13 August	Hungaroring	2nd (1:20.039)	2nd at 25.967	2nd (1:23.313)
Belgium	27 August	Spa-Francorchamps	**Pole (1:50.867)**	**1st 1:40:54.196**	2nd (2:12.890)
Italy	10 September	Monza	**Pole (1:23.720)**	Rtd (engine)	3rd (1:28.179)
Portugal	24 September	Estoril	**Pole (1:15.468)**	Rtd (acc. with Mansell)	8th (1:19.490)
Spain	1st October	Jerez	**Pole (1:20.291)**	**1st 1:47:48.264**	**FRL (1:25.779)**
Japon	22 October	Suzuka	**Pole (1:38.041)**	Disqualified	**FRL (1:43.025)**
Australia	5 November	Adelaïde	**Pole (1:16.665)**	Rtd (acc. with Brundle)	4th (1:41.159)

Position in world championship:
2nd / 60 points
Laps in lead: 487

13 pole positions, 6 wins, 4 fastest race laps
Kilometres in lead: 2301

Average points per race for season: 3.75

1990 _McLaren MP4/5B-Honda RA 100E V10

Pneus Goodyear

United States	11 March	Phoenix	5th (1:29.431)	**1st 1:52:32.829**	3rd (1:32.178)
Brazil	25 March	Interlagos	**Pole (1:17.277)**	3rd at 37.722	3rd (1:20.067)
San Marino	13 May	Imola	**Pole (1:23.220)**	Rtd (R /R wheel broken)	14th (1:30.615)
Monaco	27 May	Monaco	**Pole (1:21.314)**	**1st 1:52:46:982**	**FRL (1:24.245)**
Canada	10 June	Montréal-Notre Dame	**Pole (1:20.399)**	**1st 1:42:56:400**	5th (1:23.375)
Mexico	24 June	Mexico	3rd (1:17.670)	Rtd (R/R tyre)	6th (1:19.062)
France	8 July	Paul-Ricard	3rd (1:04.549)	3rd at 11.606	6th (1:08.573)
Great Britain	15 July	Silverstone	2nd (1:08.071)	3rd at 43.088	5th (1:12.250)
Germany	29 July	Hockenheim	**Pole (1:40.198)**	**1st 1:20:47.164**	2nd (1:45.711)
Hungary	12 August	Hungaroring	4th (1:18.162)	2nd at 0.288	5th (1:22.577)
Belgium	26 August	Spa-Francorchamps	**Pole (1:50.365)**	**1st 1:26:31.997**	2nd (1:55.132)
Italy	9 September	Monza	**Pole (1:22.533)**	**1st 1:17:57.878**	**FRL (1:26.254)**
Portugal	23 September	Estoril	3rd (1:13.601)	2nd at 2.808	6th (1:18.936)
Spain	30 September	Jerez	**Pole (1:18.387)**	Rtd (radiator)	12th (1:27.430)
Japon	21 October	Suzuka	**Pole (1:36.996)**	Rtd (accident with Prost)	–
Australia	4 November	Adelaïde	**Pole (1:15.661)**	Rtd (accident)	3rd (1:19.302)

Position in world championship:
World Champion / 78 points
Laps in lead: 556

10 pole positions, 6 wins, 2 fastest race laps
Kilometres in lead: 2493

Average points per race for season: 4.875

1991 _McLaren MP4/6-Honda RA 121E V12

Pneus Goodyear

United States	10 March	Phoenix	**Pole (1:21.434)**	**1st 2:00:47.828**	4th (1:27.153)
Brazil	24 March	Interlagos	**Pole (1:16.392)**	**1st 1:38:28:128**	3rd (1:20.841)
San Marino	28 April	Imola	**Pole (1:21.877)**	**1st 1:35:14:750**	2nd (1:27.168)
Monaco	12 May	Monaco	**Pole (1:20.344)**	**1st 1v53:02:334**	5th (1:25.250)
Canada	2nd June	Montréal-Notre Dame	3rd (1:20.318)	Rtd (electrical)	10th (1:24.647)
Mexico	24 June	Mexico	3rd (1:17.264)	3rd at 57.356	3rd (1:18.570)
France	8 July	Magny-Cours	3rd (1:14.857)	3rd at 5.416	5th (1:20.570)
Great Britain	15 July	Silverstone	2nd (1:21.618)	4th at 1 lap	4th (1:27.509)
Germany	29 July	Hockenheim	2nd (1:37.274)	7th at 1 lap	5th (1:44.213)
Hungary	12 August	Hungaroring	**Pole (1:16.147)**	**1st 1:49:12.796**	2nd (1:22.392)
Belgium	26 August	Spa-Francorchamps	**Pole (1:47.811)**	**1st 1:27:17.669**	5th (1:56.471)
Italy	9 September	Monza	**Pole (1:21.114)**	2nd at 16.262	**FRL (1:26.061)**
Portugal	23 September	Estoril	3rd (1:13.444)	2nd at 20.941	4th (1:18.929)
Spain	30 September	Barcelona-Cataluña	3rd (1:19.064)	5th at 1:02.402	7th (1:24.771)
Japon	21 October	Suzuka	2nd (1:34.898)	2nd at 0.344	**FRL (1:41.532)**
Australia	4 November	Adelaïde	**Pole (1:14.041)**	**1st 24:34.899**	2nd (1:42.545)

Position in world championship:
World Champion / 96 points
Laps in lead: 467

8 pole positions, 7 wins, 2 fastest race laps
Kilometres in lead: 2065

Average points per race for season: 6

1992 __McLaren MP4/6B-Honda RA 122E/B V12 in South Africa and in Mexico
McLaren MP4/7-Honda RA 122E/B V12 from Brazil to Australia   Tyres Goodyear

Sou^th Africa	1st March	Kyalami	2nd (1:16.227)	3rd at 34.675	2nd (1:18.140)
Mexico	22 March	Mexico	6th (1:18.791)	Rtd (transmission)	13th (1:20.721)
Brazil	5 April	Interlagos	3rd (1:17.902)	Rtd (electrical)	2nd (1:27.168)
Spain	31 May	Barcelona-Cataluña	3rd (1:21.209)	9th at 3 laps	5th (1:43.176)
San Marino	17 May	Imola	3rd (1:23.086)	3rd at 57.356	3rd (1:23.470)
Monaco	31 May	Monaco	3rd (1:20.608)	**1st 1:50:59.372**	3rd (1:23.470)
Canada	14 June	Montréal-Notre Dame	**Pole (1:16.147)**	Rtd (electrical)	6th (1:23.728)
France	5 July	Magny-Cours	3rd (1:15.199)	Rtd (acc. Schumacher)	-
Great Britain	12 July	Silverstone	3rd (1:21.706)	Rtd (gearbox)	5th (1:25.825)
Germany	26 July	Hockenheim	3rd (1:39.106)	2nd at 4.500	2nd (1:42.272)
Hungary	16 August	Hungaroring	3rd (1:16.267)	**1st 1:46:19.216**	3rd (1:19.588)
Belgium	30 August	Spa-Francorchamps	2nd (1:52.743)	5th at 1:08.369	2nd (1:54.088)
Italy	13 September	Monza	2nd (1:22.822)	**1st 1:18:15.349**	5th (1:27.190)
Portugal	27 September	Estoril	3rd (1:14.258)	3rd at 1 lap	**FRL (1:16.272)**
Japon	25 October	Suzuka	3rd (1:38.375)	Rtd (engine)	**FRL (1:41.532)**
Australia	8 November	Adelaïde	2nd (1:14.202)	Rtd (acc. with Mansell)	2nd (1:42.545)

Position in world championship:
4th / 50 points
Laps in lead: 95

1 pole position, 3 wins, 2 fastest race laps
Kilometres in lead: 415

Average points per race for season: 3.125

1993 __McLaren MP4/8-Ford Cosworth HB V8   Pneus Goodyear

South Africa	14 March	Kyalami	2nd (1:15.784)	2nd at 1:19.824	6th (1:20.755)
Brazil	28 March	Interlagos	6th (1:17.697)	**1st 1:51:15.485**	2nd (1:20.187)
Europe	11 April	Donington Park	4th (1:12.107)	**1st 1:50:46.570**	**FRL (1:18.029)**
San Marino	25 April	Imola	4th (1:24.007)	Rtd (suspension)	3rd (1:27.490)
Spain	9 May	Barcelona-Cataluña	3rd (1:19.722)	2nd at 16.873	2nd (1:21.717)
Monaco	23 May	Monaco	3rd (1:21.552)	**1st 1:52:10.947**	3rd (1:23.737)
Canada	13 June	Montréal-Notre Dame	8th (1:21.706)	Rtd (alternator)	3rd (1:22.015)
France	4 July	Magny-Cours	5th (1:16.264)	4th at 32.405	3rd (1:20.521)
Great Britain	11 July	Silverstone	4th (1:21.986)	5th at 1 lap	5th (1:24.886)
Germany	25 July	Hockenheim	4th (1:39.616)	4th at 1:08.229	2nd (1:42.162)
Hungary	15 August	Hungaroring	4th (1:16.451)	Rtd (throttle)	13th (1:22.838)
Belgium	29 August	Spa-Francorchamps	5th (1:49.934)	4th at 1:39.763	5th (1:54.185)
Italy	12 September	Monza	4th (1:22.633)	Rtd (acc. with Brundle)	9th (1:27.939)
Portugal	26 September	Estoril	4th (1:12.491)	Rtd (engine)	15th (1:18.365)
Japon	24 October	Suzuka	2nd (1:37.284)	**1st 1:40:27.912**	4th (1:43.217)
Australia	7 November	Adelaïde	**Pole (1:13.371)**	**1st 1:43:27.476**	3rd (1:16.128)

Position in world championship:
2nd / 73 points
Laps in lead: 424

1 pole position, 5 wins, 1 fastest race lap
Kilometres in lead: 2054

Average points per race for season: 4.562

1994 __Williams FW16- Renault RS6 V10   Tyres Goodyear

Brazil	27 March	Interlagos	**Pole (1:15.962)**	Rtd (accident)	2nd (1:18.764)
Pacific	17 April	Ti-Aïda	**Pole (1:10.218)**	Rtd (acc. with Häkkinen)	-
San Marino	1st May	Imola	**Pole (1:21.548)**	Rtd (accident)	22nd (1:44.068)

Position in world championship:
Not classified
Laps in lead: 36

3 poles position
Kilometres in lead: 103

Average points per race for season: 0

_INDEX

_ACKNOWLEDGEMENTS

The author would like to thank for their precious accounts and other help: Gerhard Berger, Marc Boulineau, Fabrice Connen, Gérard Ducarouge, Pierre Dupasquier, Lionel Froissart, Jacques Laffite, Max Mosley, Gordon Murray, Henri Pescarolo, Alain Prost, Clare Robertson (TAG McLaren), Serena Santolamazza (Renault-Sport), Jonathan Williams (Williams F1).

_BIBLIOGRAPHY

"Ayrton Senna, itinéraire d'un enfant gâté"
Lionel Froissart – Ed. Glénat

"Ayrton Senna, Au fil du temps"
Christopher Hilton – Ed. Chronosports

The annuals *"Autocourse"* and *"L'Année Formule 1"*

The magazines *"Auto-Hebdo"* and *"Sport-Auto"*